# Pages from Grandma's Notebooks

## Selected Essays and Poems

## LEONA FLOWERS

ISBN: 978-1-6847-1146-8 (sc)
ISBN: 978-1-6847-1147-5 (hc)
ISBN: 978-1-6847-1145-1 (e)

Library of Congress Control Number: 2019915891

Lulu Publishing Services rev. date: 01/28/2020

This little book represents a collection of my memories
and thoughts to inspire you toward hope, strength,
and discovering your own reasons for joy.

# *Foreword*

From the time I was a little boy, I knew my Grandmother, or "Mup" as I call her, was special. I realized that the relationship between grandparent and grandchild was a sacred one; where two people, separated by nearly half a century in birthdays could share in stories of one's hard-lived experiences, and the other's seemingly new beginnings.

My Grandmother would always ask me to tell her something she didn't know. It was her way of not only engaging in my studies at school, my young adult life and now into my early thirties, but also, to enlighten her own inner student of the world and the people living in it.

My grandmother humorously refers to herself as a "Youth Vampire", always wanting to stay connected to the vitality of "young people", so she can stay, as Bob Dylan would say "Forever Young"

Going to her house with my sister, Dana, when we were kids, was like going to "The Great American Summer Camp" where the soda flowed like from a garden hose and fried egg sandwiches were always on the house. And whether we were walking down the nearby railroad track singing songs of days gone by, or going down to the basement in her house to watch old "Bud Abbott and Lou Costello" films, or sitting around the coffee table playing cards—always referring to the "Book of Hoyle" if there were any disputes— spending time with my Mup was always a special occasion.

Her laugh should be recorded and preserved in film, for it can bring a smile to anyone upon hearing it. It is both infectious and contagious.

She is both a master storyteller and story listener. When someone speaks, her ability to listen, absorb and retain allows her to ponder, reflect and relate to just about anybody in the world. I know, because I've seen it.

When I was a boy, I loved to sit on my Grandmother's lap and listen as she told me stories that would transport me back to her days as a very poor child growing up on a farm with her pet pig named "Sally", or picking blackberries from the bushes with her mother, or how she loved riding along in a horse and wagon with her dear old Irish father, and my great grandfather, Jimmy Dean.......and many more, some of which you will soon read in this book.

Yes, I always knew my Mup was special. Because of that, I never felt right about keeping her all to myself. Over the years she has become a Grandmother to many of my friends, my wife, Keleigh, countless "strangers" along the way, and now, to all of you. It is my honor and my privilege to share with you my Mup... Slainte!

—Miles Teller, *Beloved grandson of Leona and Jesse Flowers and reigning Gin Rummy Champion*

The author with her grandson, Hollywood actor, Miles Teller

# Preface

I've been jotting down my thoughts and memories in notebooks for a long time. Many of them remain stacked on shelves in my house. I even have one I've held onto since grammar school. I didn't stop using hard copy notebooks when I got my first computer because I can get thoughts out easier writing by hand. There's a certain artistry about it that connects you to writers of the past. But there came a point when I did begin to copy some of the material contained in my notebooks onto my computer. Some of what this book contains is from those old paper notebooks and some is from the new technology I've employed.

When I was strongly urged more recently, in conversation with friends whose opinion I highly valued, that I overcome my hesitancy and begin to compose a book sharing those influences and perceptions that have shaped my life, I thought perhaps now the time had come to try. So, I started scouring my material, both old and not so old, for what I might include that would be of interest or practical use to readers. I enlisted my husband's help.

It has been said that our spouse is to be our help mate. No one has fit that role better than my beloved husband of fifty-six years, Jesse. He has aided me to the extent of often being awakened from his sleep, poor man, to listen to something for which I needed his assistance or advice. Or maybe just a listening ear. He always rose to the occasion.

Our children, Merry, Brian and Jesse, Jr., have also been urging me for many years to write a book. They are each now middle-aged, so we have been by each other's side in both joy and much sorrow. They are not only my children but are also my friends and confidantes. Because I value their opinions I've listened when they've individually suggested I should attempt to create something along the lines of what they've observed me doing from their earliest memories-sharing my personal stories and speaking on subjects that they are aware has helped motivate others- toward making wiser choices, growing, trusting heaven and discovering their own inner strengths and talents. That is what I've sought to do with this little book.

But there is another purpose to my efforts in this book. As the title suggests I'm attempting to leave behind a grandmother's voice in messages I hope will be of value to my own descendants.

Jesse and I have been blessed with several generations of grandchildren. What an immeasurable joy they have brought to our lives. Their ranks currently number twenty-four, and growing. They range in age from newborn to forty-plus. The older grandchildren have often warmed my heart by telling me they feel fortunate in having had me in their lives. They can recall, they tell me, advice or support which I've provided for addressing almost any circumstance of life. They've hoped that through composing a book I would share just some of the grandmotherly wisdom they've enjoyed with an audience who, perhaps, have lost or never knew what it was to have a grandmother. My grandchildren's special love, contributions and encouragement has been elevating to my spirit.

I would be amiss if I didn't take this opportunity to say a special thank you to my grandson, Miles Teller, whose celebrity has helped popularize me and provided me with so many opportunities to know and be known. His love and pride in me have been invaluable in providing that extra push of confidence.

This first work of mine-PAGES FROM GRANDMA'S NOTEBOOKS- is also offered to the enormous number of family and friends in my circle of love who have known me well for years. They have been steadfast in their belief that mine is an experience and perspective worth sharing and have repeatedly asked that I please put ink to page and do so. Now I have.

*Leona Flowers*
Zephyrhills, Florida
2019

Your words have power.
Speak words that are kind, loving, positive,
uplifting, encouraging, and life-giving.

—Author unknown

# Contents

# 1

## Time and Tea Leaves

A man without mirth is like a wagon without springs.
—H. W. Beecher

Once upon a time, I met some gypsies. They were not like the ones you see in storybooks. They were very kind to me when I needed kindness, and they made me laugh when I needed laughter.

I can still see the little shack the gypsies lived in, sitting alongside the road going toward the town of Salem, New Jersey. If it weren't for the old cars occasionally parked there, it would have been hard for average folks to believe that anyone lived there.

Behind it, tall reeds grew along Salem Creek. There was no yard, per se, just a lot of muddy ground that you slopped through to get to the shack.

It had been built, who knows when, from lumber scratched up here and there, surely before the days of building codes or any of today's laws about the number of persons who can occupy a certain amount of space.

The outside of the shack was covered with linoleum, scrounged from the dump next to the Mannington Mills Flooring Co. The products this company produces today go by many names, but back in 1951, everyone just called the stuff "linoleum." Poor people, like most of the folks I knew, found it versatile. Necessity and imagination could put it to a lot of uses.

The folks who lived in that little shack had nailed—and re-nailed—layer after layer of the linoleum over the wooden frame they'd somehow constructed. Then they latticed wood over the top of the linoleum to keep the wind from blowing it off.

Then there was the roof of the building, which was covered with four-foot-by-eight-foot sheets of corrugated tin. Whenever it rained, the noise on the tin roof was so loud that you could hardly hear someone talking even if they were sitting right next to you.

Poking up through the tin roof was a section of galvanized chimney pipe that was connected to a little stove that was positioned in the house below. When finances allowed, it burned either wood or coal, but in especially tough times, corncobs were burned in it as well.

After all these years, I'm amazed that I can still see that little black stove sitting there. It was a small, oval-shaped stove, with a lift-off lid for inserting heating material. It was vital. It represented the only source of heat and the single means of cooking, so something was always sitting on top of it. It might be a simple meal from a soup bone and whatever else was on hand to throw in the pot—or it might be just water boiling in a teakettle to pour over reused coffee grounds. If nothing was cooking on top of the stove, then a galvanized bucket of water was often kept there, just in case someone had a need to bathe or launder something.

In the warmer months of the year, the family ate a lot of sandwiches, deli foods, or fish they'd caught in the creek behind them.

I recall they had an improvised "grill" constructed of concrete blocks they'd found somewhere or had been given. Their poverty encouraged a boldness on their part. If they saw something sitting unused, they wouldn't hesitate to ask, "Hey, are you gonna' use that?"

They often found that folks would have a little sympathy and say, "No, you can go ahead and take it."

I was entertained by their inventions. They were adaptable to circumstances. I liked that about them. I suspected they had survival lessons to teach to an observant girl like myself.

No family member was ever turned away, no matter how far the little band had to stretch their resources. Sometimes, their small dwelling was cramped, to say the least, when others had fallen onto even worse times.

The sleeping areas were defined by pieces of clothesline strung from wall to wall, with sheets or blankets hanging over the line for a semblance of privacy. I have no idea what served as a bed for any of them because I never saw behind the "curtains."

Set back a short distance from the shack, toward the creek, sat an outhouse constructed from similar materials. I never used it for fear of snakes from the creek getting cozy in there. Older Sears Roebuck catalogs were taken in there to be used as toilet paper.

I recall a big table set somewhere in the center of the room where everyone loosely gathered, sitting on chairs with no backs or on upturned wooden crates. Coffee cups, some without handles or with chips in them, sat about with varying amounts of dark brew in them. Saltine crackers lay open on the table—something solid to dip in the coffee.

Among all these memories, it's strange how I recall the old dog that the folks had taken in. In my thinking, it seemed a foolish choice for him to seek to join them. He surely would have been a whole lot better off if he had just kept on wandering down the road. But he seemed to enjoy all the petting he received from the family and their friends. He seemed content. Thin, but content. I suppose even animals will take food for the heart over physical nourishment.

It's been many years now, and you would think it all would have faded from my mind. Yet those pleasant recollections linger still.

I can recall their faces even now.

There was the lady with the gentle eyes whose name was Nation. She was not very attractive and seemed old to me at my young age. Now I realize she couldn't have been more than in her late thirties because she had two young daughters: Sophie, who was nineteen, and Etta, who was sixteen. I had a special affection for Nation because she had a natural kindness.

Then there was Peter, Nation's younger brother. I liked Peter because he was always laughing. I've always been drawn to happy personalities. Peter seemed to have that thing about him that induces others to smile.

And I can't forget the handsome, curly-haired cousin, Willie, who seemed to delight in telling stories about his escapades with the ladies he met in some of the local nightspots. Sometimes Nation would have to remind him that I was listening to his stories.

"Well, she's a pretty little gal, and she's gonna' run into fellas like me someday, so she needs to know how we operate," he laughingly said one time. The rest turned their eyes on me and laughed along with Willie. I covered my grinning face. Willie had just said I was pretty, and that mattered a lot to my ragamuffin self.

The atmosphere that surrounded the gypsies in that little house was one of continuous conversation and lighthearted argument. Sometimes, someone would bring a guitar and play it. On those nights, there might be some singing. But always the social gatherings would at some point include exaggerated tales about one another, which never failed to elicit peals of laughter. I guess it was the laughter under those harsh circumstances that held my fascination with them.

I began going to the gypsies' house with my big brother, Tommy, who had met and been charmed by the chunky, red-haired, outrageous Sophie—Nation's elder daughter. The smiling Sophie was everything my poor brother was not. She was like sunshine to his rain, and he obviously enjoyed her boldness and the humor she seemed to find in everything. Fortunately for me, he sometimes would let me tag along when he went to see her.

Looking back, I'm certain Tommy didn't harbor any illusions that it would ever be any more than it was for him right then. But at least it was *something* in his otherwise dreary life.

I have no idea where my brother met Sophie, but I'd bet that it was *she* who introduced herself to him somewhere. His vulnerability was obvious to anyone, as was his kindness.

I'm sure he knew their relationship couldn't and wouldn't last long, and it appeared that he soaked up the moments like a dry sponge.

I was only a child, but I had a sense that my poor brother was having one put over on him by Sophie. I didn't have the heart to tell him. I mentioned my feelings to our mom, but she said for me not to get into big folks' business. She reminded me that Tommy was a grown man who could do as he pleased.

Be that as it may, I just knew that, despite her humorous hugs and an occasional sitting on his lap as the others laughed and joked about their romance, my brother's real appeal to Sophie was his monthly military disability check.

When the first of each month came around, Tommy would get cleaned up and head for the gypsies' little house. When he took me along, I had an idea of how the evening would proceed.

Up to a certain point in the process, there would be the usual talk and laughter. Then, before long, the senior members of the clan, along with Sofie, would happily head out the door with their arms around Tommy, ushering me along with smiles.

Our merry group might end up at the grocery store, the deli, or the custard stand, all in my brother's car, naturally. And of course, Sophie would be snuggled up close to Tommy as he drove—no doubt to inspire his generosity. It was great fun for me, and Tommy would be a little lighter in his spirit on the way home.

I loved my brother and knew something about how most of his days and nights were spent. All our family lived with the physical and mental wounds Tommy had incurred storming the beach at Normandy during World War II.

He had spent months in VA hospitals following his severe injuries that historic day.

Then he had to experience the horrors from the terrible way PTSD (post-traumatic stress syndrome) was treated at that time in history—by the use of electric shock therapy and other inhumane "medical procedures." It left my brother with hands that would move and shake involuntarily. It took extreme focus for him to do the simplest things. Needless to say, he got frustrated and upset very easily. He suffered endless sleepless nights, confused thinking, and bouts of deep depression.

Yet he was one of those lucky ones who made it home. For those of us who loved him, his place in our midst was something for which to be grateful. My older sister, Mary, who was close in age to Tommy growing up, told me that, as a boy, he had always been a bit shy and not very forward with girls. So, looking back, I guess, for him, the cost of some groceries, a movie, or a little beer wasn't too high a price to pay for evenings that would otherwise have been spent in anxious loneliness. On those occasions, it was a pleasant sight for me to see my big brother smile or laugh.

I feel I should mention that I never heard, as a child—or since for that matter—that any of those gypsies ever stole anything from anyone or otherwise caused anyone any harm. With that said, I'm positive they charmed quite a few folks into parting willingly with their money. Because you see, it was always, "let's go here" or "let's do" such-and-such. They included *you* in the fun—the eating and drinking, the trip to the movie theater, or whatever "pony ride" they had in mind. But of course, it went without saying that the going and the doing would be with *your* money.

I know fate meant for me to meet those wonderful people who, for a brief spell in my young life, supplied me with insights I would not otherwise have gained: people who provided flavor and color to my experience. I'm grateful for what Sophie and Tommy's friendship gave to me in that difficult era of my own young life.

When Tommy was visiting in the little shack with Sophie and the other gypsies there, I sometimes liked to wander over next door to visit with "the grandmother." She was a sweet, whitehaired lady, who lived in a small, neat trailer. Out in front of her trailer, close to the highway where passersby could see, there hung a sign on which the words were neatly stenciled: "Palms Read, Fortunes Told, Tea Leaves Read."

And right there in the center, between the words, was a huge picture of a hand—a *big* hand with all the fingers pointing right straight up in the air! To an imaginative kid like me, it appeared to be extending the greeting "how" that Indians gave to the "white man" in all the cowboy-and-Indian movies I had seen.

Now, I admit I really didn't know what that hand was all about, but I was very impressed by that sign. That was a *business sign*, and no one I knew had a business sign.

The grandmother had a small group of regular clients who believed in and sought the comfort of her "gift" of insight they believed she possessed and from which she provided them advice on personal and emotional matters. It was her customer's "love contributions" for her "readings" that no doubt brought in most of the income that kept the whole family going.

On occasion, when there were none of her clients' cars parked out front, I would go over and visit with the grandmother. I was always full of questions, and with her patient good humor, she would try her best to answer them.

She wasn't a "schooled" woman, as she would tell me, but heaven had let her "know things," she said. And I believed she did. I believed she was different from all the rest of us. I wished so much that I could be like her and know things too.

I liked the grandmother, and I could tell she liked me as well. She would fix my braids if they came undone or make me some tea with her cookies. Sometimes when I was there, she would send me on the errand of walking down to the local bait and tackle store to get some chewing tobacco for her. You didn't have to be of any age back then to buy tobacco, and kids were often sent to the stores to buy it. I was glad to do it! Because when she sent me, she would always give me a little extra change to buy something sweet for myself.

I remember one day when I was looking down into a cup at what I just knew were her magic tea leaves, that I got up the nerve to ask the grandmother if she would please tell me something about what my future would be like. I had no money, but I thought perhaps for friendship, she might oblige me.

Nothing in my life contained a flicker of promise. The future was blank, and my mother had not a clue to offer me except to say that I should study hard in school and then perhaps I would have more than she did. Everything was just a day-to-day struggle. So, from all I'd observed, I suspected that my prospects weren't very encouraging.

But perhaps the grandmother could see what my Mom and I couldn't.

When I asked her the question, the grandmother just looked at me for a minute with what I knew was great consideration. Then, she reached across the table and patted my hand. She knew about my widowed mother, my deceased father, and my hard life. She shook her head back and forth as she began to speak to me.

I was certain that whatever she was about to say would be very important, so I listened intently as she spoke. This is my best and most honest recollection of her message to me that day:

"Honey," she began, "I don't need to read anything from your teacup to know how you're going to live your life. I can tell you're a real smart little gal, and you got a brightness about you. You're good, and you're strong, and you're going to be able to handle anything that comes your way. Life may get hard sometimes, but you're going to figure out how to get through it all. I always know when folks are weak and foolish and when they're wise, and I can tell that you're a whole lot wiser than any of those big folks that come in here. I see you watching everything, so I know you'll learn a lot from what you see and hear, and I got a feeling that nobody's going to put anything over on you. You aren't going to need anybody to tell you which way to go. You'll make your own way just fine. So, don't worry. You'll be okay. Now, you go on. I'm going to lay down awhile."

I gave the grandmother a long hug and held onto her for an extra moment for some reason. Then I left, feeling a whole lot less fearful than when I had entered her home.

No matter what others might have believed about the grandmother's gifts, they could not have convinced me she did not have a special vision of things. I was positive there were things she knew.

Looking back, I can see where the grandmother was right about a lot of things where my life was concerned. I *have* sought education and wisdom, I *have* handled everything life has thrown at me, I *do* understand human motivation very well, and I *have* learned what cripples people and what inspires them. So, she gave me an honest reading that day.

Sadly, and strangely, that day was the last time I saw the grandmother. She died shortly after that, and without her help, the rest of the clan in the little shack eventually moved on to other places. The trailer was sold, the shack was torn down, and the spot where the laughter had lived for a while reverted to mud and reeds.

That was also the end of Tommy and Sofie. Of course, they parted as friends. For years to come, he always would get happy whenever he spoke of Sophie and all his old friends, the gypsies.

As the years passed, I would occasionally run into one or two of the family, and we would exchange our news of what time and circumstances were doing to affect each of our lives. They would sometimes mention with a smile that I was growing into such a nice young lady—and how pretty I had become. We would part with a hug and the hope that we would see each other again soon. But life took its twists and turns, and all our lives took different paths. Those few brief days of my youth soon became just pleasant memories.

I've never been embarrassed to say that I've been happy for those hours spent in the gypsies' little circle, of riding to the custard stand in my brother Tommy's old car loaded with cheerful people, and of smelling the coffee while sitting around a little black stove and listening to the sound of a guitar.

Whenever I have ever thought of those olden days, I have never been able to recall a single tear or weary sigh in those gatherings. In all the scenes that still leap to my mind, I am only reminded of smiling faces. It never cost me a single dime to laugh with the gypsies.

They're all gone now, but I wish somehow that I could thank them for teaching me some very valuable life lessons—about how family and friendship and love that is generous can carry you through an awful lot of tough times.

My brother Tommy before deployment in WWll

# 2
# Love and a Carousel

I can remember a time, when I was a small child around six years old, that my father told me he had a surprise for me. He said he would be taking me someplace that would make me very happy. The whole family was going. Mother would make up a lunch basket, we would catch a bus, and we would spend a whole day there. I can remember the excitement my father created in me that day. It would turn out to be even beyond my childish expectations.

On the Delaware River in Pennsville, New Jersey, there was a wonderful place known as Riverview Beach Park. It was a very popular amusement park that attracted folks from all over the tri-state area, which included Delaware and Pennsylvania.

Several ferries traveled back and forth daily across the river from Philadelphia and Wilmington, Delaware, bringing summer crowds to the park. Buses from towns around South Jersey like the one we traveled on from our town of Salem, dropped off passengers right in front of the entrance to the park.

It was childhood heaven! As soon as you got off the bus, you heard the music. You heard the sounds of people screaming as they rode the roller coaster. And the smells were a conglomerate of hot dogs, French fries, cotton candy, and almost everything else that get the gastric juices flowing.

It was not a place I ever wanted to leave. My father smiled broadly down at me, and my eyes must have told him how thrilled he had made his little girl. In an era long before Disney World, my father had brought me to the dwelling place of childhood joy and magic.

I remember the first time I gazed at a merry-go-round. I would love them for the rest of my life.

Mom set up a picnic table, but probably for the first time, I was not hungry.

At some point, my father went to a little red booth and bought a string of tickets as long as my arm. Then he took my hand and led me to the carousel. It was housed in the most beautiful circular building with paintings all over and played its own special music that was at the speed of the horses as they moved up and down on a pole. I was mesmerized.

"Pick the pony you want to ride, Sis," my dad urged. "Hurry up, before it starts to move. Daddy will get off, but I'll be watching you from over there." Then he pointed to a bench under a shade tree that I could see each time I circled the room.

"Each time the fellow comes around, you hand him one of your tickets," he said as he placed me on my chosen stallion. I was so excited that I was shaking. I gripped the pole and straightened myself in the saddle. I was riding on my own magical horse to the strains of delightful music in this fairy-tale place. It was pure joy.

I can't say I know exactly what I was thinking as I rode 'round and 'round with my hand filled with tickets. I'm sure I waved to my father on each turn, and I'm sure he returned each delighted wave of my hand.

I will never forget that moment in my young life, what I felt riding on a merry-go-round for the first time, or the smile on my father's face as he watched me.

That day, from start to finish, lives on in my happiest memories. I fell asleep in my father's arms on the bus ride home.

I went to Riverview Beach Park many times over the years, and I later took my own children there. I will always remember when my father planned a day just for me that did not disappoint even the best of my most wonderful childhood dreams—to a place where I forever fell in love with a carousel and those beautiful painted ponies.

# 3
# *The Easter Collar*

My mother and I shared a unique bond because, like her, I had also lost my father. She had lost hers at twenty-six, and I had lost mine at only ten, so I was always aware of the sympathy she had for me.

"Don't think you can abuse her just because she doesn't have a father," Mom would say to my older siblings, all fathered by her first husband, a man who had been demanding and cruel to both her and their children. They were all grown by then, except for Grace, who was almost seventeen and still lived at home.

My mother said she was now the only protector that her small girl had left in the world, and she was not going to allow anyone, especially my own brothers and sisters, to be unkind to me.

I know it was from this special connection, as the only child she'd had with the only man she'd ever loved, that so much of her sacrifice for me sprung.

It was three weeks before Easter, 1952, and I had spent many hours perusing the only view of the fashion world to which my young mind had access: the Sears Roebuck catalog. My mom had brought home the special Easter edition, and for a kid as poor as I was, it was where dreams were conjured. Wonderland!

It didn't take long before I knew everything that was in that Sears Roebuck Special Easter Edition—from the varieties of baby chickens they could ship to you with a guarantee of no loss to the fancy dresses made for the stylish young girl.

As my dazzled eyes scanned page after page of girl's clothing, searching with some new urge for something that had the magic built into each stitch and would change me from ordinary to extraordinary, my gaze finally froze on one image! My young mind lapsed into immediate overwhelming longings. There it was—the most beautiful outfit my young eyes had ever seen. It was a pink bouclé skirt that zippered in the back and a waist-length pink poodle cloth cape that went with it. (The white nylon blouse was not included).

Up until then, my mom had always carefully selected and purchased clothing and footwear for Grace and me based on her meager income. Until that day, I had never considered making any requests. That came to an end that Easter season.

I was eleven years old at the time, but closer to twelve. Perhaps my age was to blame, but I couldn't take my mind off that two-piece bouclé suit. I looked at it every single day and thought about how glamorous it would make me look when I walked into Alloway Baptist Church on Easter Sunday completed, of course, with shiny black Mary Jane shoes, the white blouse shown with the outfit and new white gloves and hat. I envisioned everyone turning and looking at me as I made my entrance. I just had to have that moment. And so, my whining to my mother began.

I was successful. The day came when Mom went to the Sears Roebuck store in town and picked up her order. My outfit was finally here. As soon as she entered the house with the package, I hurried it upstairs, hung it up, and stared. It was even more beautiful than I had imagined, and I couldn't wait until Easter morning when I would have my Cinderella moment.

Finally, Easter morning dawned. I made my entrance down the stairs like a princess, in my mind. I looked around for approval from Mom and Grace. Mom had a pleased smile, but when I looked closer at her, I noticed she was wearing her very same old church dress that she had worn for so long, onto which now she had sewn a new dime-store collar over the old frayed one. I was confused. This wasn't the way it was supposed to be. We were all supposed to be in new Easter clothes, walking into church today.

"Where's your new Easter dress, Mommy?" I asked, distressed at her appearance.

"Oh, this one still has lots of wear left in it," she said with a smile. "And you look lovely, honey. You were right. It's just what you should have."

In that moment, I didn't feel very lovely because a nagging feeling had crept into my conscience.

Grace leaned in close to me and spoke what I feared was the truth into my ear: "She spent so much of the Easter money on you that she couldn't afford a new dress for herself. How pretty do you feel now, you selfish thing?"

My mother immediately chastised Grace and rushed to comfort me. My mother understood how my fantasies helped me escape from the harshness of life, yet those feelings of guilt were especially hard to bear. I began to cry. Any satisfaction with myself that I had been feeling earlier shriveled up like bacon in a hot pan. In its place was a heart filled with pain.

My mother drew me to her and lifted my chin as she spoke to me that day. She told me that she realized she had few opportunities to make me happy. When she realized how much that outfit seemed to mean to me, she wanted me to have it as well. She told me she knew that childhood passes quickly and that there would be other days in my life and other Easters where I might not be as happy as I had been awaiting that day.

A dress for herself was just a dress she told me, but seeing me so happy had made that Easter day extra special for her too. If I cried and felt bad, well, then, she would lose her happiness too.

She ended by comforting me with her certainty that when I grew up, a day would come when I could buy her new dresses in return—and wouldn't that be nice for both of us? It was an opportunity that my young heart longed for in that moment as badly as it had longed for that pink Easter outfit.

She lived long enough for me keep my promise, and I always did so with an eager, happy heart. Until the day she left this world at the age of eighty-three, I was dedicated to making my mother happy. I would make up holidays just to bring her smiles with my gifts.

I responded to every request she ever made of me and tried never to disappoint a mother who had done so much to teach me kindness.

It's been more than sixty years since that Easter morning of my childhood, yet I have never forgotten that profound moment in my life and the example of sacrificial love that I was shown by my mother's dime-store collar.

Leona behind her mother in 1949

# 4
# *Us as Stardust*

It seems to me that some folks don't think very highly of who and what they are. I guess they haven't discovered how much they have within themselves to honor and appreciate. That's too bad because we humans are, as Dr. Deepak Chopra says, an amazing entity composed of "unlimited possibilities."

I agree with Dr. Chopra. I believe we're much more than we'll ever know. We're filled with unmined gold of shining potential, an inexplicable miracle with a mind that is a conduit of all the universe holds of magic and wonder. We are weavers of dreams on a human frame.

I find it fascinating to know that there is nothing—and no one—who has ever been exactly like me with my unique spirit and capabilities. No one has ever dreamed my dreams, and dreams are the catalysts that twirl and spin in our minds like magic wands and bring things into being.

So, keep dreaming. Even when others blow out the candles on your dreams, light them again. And again. As often as needed. And never close the door on the unlimited creative spirit that dwells within you or look to others to validate you. Twinkle, twinkle, little star. Sprinkle your stardust on the world.

# 5
## Mother Prayed

I can close my eyes and still hear the wind as it howled through the trees and around that old house we lived in.

There were pieces of wood missing here and there throughout its ancient frame. Its lapboard siding was probably a hundred years old, and some of the tar paper patches had blown off. After my father died, no one was around to do the many things he used to do.

During the winter following his death, there was a crack in the wall over my bed. I remember that hole being large enough that if I put my eye over the hole, I could see outside. But I didn't really want to see, because I knew what was out there: snow banked up against the side of the house, higher than my flimsy Sears Roebuck boots.

I recall how, trying to find some comfort in my bed at night, I would search with my feet for the hot brick I had taken from off the top of the potbelly stove before mom banked down the fire each winter night in order to save coal.

Even under the blankets, the brick would quickly cool down on those cold nights. I only hoped it would stay warm against my double-socked feet long enough for me to fall asleep.

Always on the darkest or coldest of nights, before I could doze off, I would hear the soft murmur of a voice. It was my mother's voice. And even though I couldn't see her, I knew that in the other bedroom, she was kneeling in prayer.

I never recall a single night of my childhood—no matter how weary or ill she might be—that my mother ever climbed into her bed without first talking to God. I sometimes felt that if she ever became unable to assume her nightly practice that I might hear some magnificent "Other" voice coming from her room saying, "Dora, are you mad at me for something? I miss our talks."

Part of the reason I was able to cope with the hardships of my own young life was that I knew, no matter how cold my dearest mother's own feet were—or how burdened her heart might be from the many cares of her day—that God would never have to wonder about the state of my mother's spirit. Because my mother always prayed.

Leona Flowers

# 6

# Keeping Fear in Its Place

Stop being afraid of life, of other people, of events we think are looming. Stop being timid and fearful of what *might* be. Fear robs us of strength and of joy.

The moment you give in to fear, it works its way into how you choose to think and act. Fear is a part of our survival mechanism. It was designed within us to help keep us safe. Its function is to keep us from carelessness and folly. But when, without reason, we are full of fear that something harmful is impending, when we stay apprehensive and are prevented from fully enjoying our daily lives, then that mechanism that nature has provided us for our safety's sake is not serving us properly.

As a young woman, I would go to my mother with my concerns over what troubles might befall me and that I might not be able to handle. Life for me was still mostly an unknown. I spoke to her of my fears of meeting potential challenges and asked her how I might deal with them. I wanted her wisdom to help prepare me because I knew she had endured so many difficulties in her own life. And I was new on the path to the future.

Mom's quiet way of listening and then sharing words of wisdom and advice somehow always hit the mark. I seemed less afraid when I left her.

My mother had lived her life on simple premises: that either there was someone we could rely on to help and guide us through life—some divine parent who knew our needs and had us in their hand—or we could otherwise, through unbelief, sink into the despair of the faithless. It really was that simple for her.

Those notions and precepts of a rooted and grounded faith saw her through all life brought into her experience from early childhood to her last day. She was like a rock in a storm—never blown away by any of the fierce assaults that raged against her human frame.

I wanted her fearlessness. And so, from those days of living under the example of that spiritual Amazon who preached by the example of her courage in the face of so many struggles and pain, I eventually developed my own simple philosophy for confronting all that has come to engage my own human spirit.

My own strength came in the form of a question I knew I had to answer for myself: Did I believe that my life was led? To me, that meant I must believe that my soul would have sufficient personal revelation and inspiration to sustain me throughout my life's experiences and that I would be provided somehow with assurances that I was enjoined to a guiding, strengthening Divine Presence. If I chose to believe these things, then I should have *nothing to fear.*

But if I didn't—if I allowed myself to accept the thought that I was just some unimportant happening in an unguided, uncaring, empty universe—then, hopelessly, I would be justified in fearing *everything*!

I have chosen to believe, and have continued to believe, that despite a world filled with countless trials, tears, and dangers, that I *have* been led. And it has made all the difference in whether I fell under the load life has laid on me or not.

I've found miracles and aid in every circumstance of my life, and I have always—*always*—been led eventually to those times my mother mentioned of "good cheer."

Thank you, Mother, for pointing out the path to hopefulness and trust. I wish you could know that your lessons took.

# 7
## Mother Said

My mother used to say that a thief is a liar—and a liar is a thief. They are cut from the same moral fabric. Therefore, she said, "If someone lies to you, keep your eye on your wallet, and when someone has stolen anything from you, never believe a word they say."

# 8
# The Sayings

I grew up in a house full of sayings. They were everywhere one looked. They were on shiny blue cardboard plaques bought by my mother from door-to-door salesmen or from a rare trip to the five-and-dime store. She hung them all over the walls of our shabby old house as reminders to reach a little deeper, try a little harder, and believe in Something Higher.

Mom also placed value on quotes from folks she regarded as of high moral stature. There were hundreds of these quotes she felt worthy of being saved and repeated—cut or torn from newspapers and magazines and stuffed in her Bible or other books she valued. I had to handle all her books with care lest tons of scraps of paper would fall out all over the floor and have to be gathered up.

Those plaques she purchased were hung over my bed and in every doorway it seemed. I recall one that she placed on the bureau next to my bed to greet me with a message of faith when I opened my eyes each day. It stated: "You don't need to know what the future holds if you know Who holds the future."

Sayings were the *stuffing* of my young psyche.

Whatever my mother felt that these items lacked in providing an instant philosophy for me, she would supplement with tales of her youth and her laudable upbringing by her good Christian father, Thomas, and his sister, Anna. Though never having met them, somehow, through my mom, I felt that I had. "My father would always say," and "My aunt Anna would always say" were substantially supplied by my mother to complete my curriculum of Sayings 101.

The wall plaques contained sayings such as these:

- Where there's a will, there's a way.
- God helps those who help themselves.
- Time changes everything.
- Let every tub stand on its own bottom.
- Change what you can, accept what you can't, and know the difference.

Brief statements of this latter sort seen each day were powerful incentives to a kid like me, toward living a life of perseverance and self-sufficiency and having faith in a God who wanted you to be a winner.

From an early age, when I began sharing my philosophy with them, adults looked at me with appreciation for my wholesome influences. However, if they knew my mother, they weren't very surprised. She was regarded as a woman of faith, pride, strength, and honesty.

My knowledge helped make me a cheerful kid despite my existence in the midst of great poverty. I was never in a situation where I couldn't look around and find one of my mother's plaques with some wisdom or advice that applied. I discovered lessons for a lifetime on my mother's broken plaster walls and in her accumulated positive thoughts—lessons in the power of gratitude, self-reliance, unrelenting faith, and the relativity of happiness.

In tough times, like when there was no money at all and the cupboard was low, my mother would say, "Only so much food fills the belly, whether it's meat and potatoes or just bread and tea." So, with what she could scrape together, she would make us a loaf of bread.

We would wait until the bread cooled and then slap our slices of bread onto the side of the old potbelly stove that supplied our only source of heat. When necessary, it also served as an adequate toaster. We'd keep our eyes on the toasting process, and when we figured our slices were brown enough, we would unstick them with a fork, flip them over, and toast their other side. When our dinner of bread was ready, we would fold the bread over and dip it into a cup of plain, often unsweetened tea. To a hungry kid, it was a feast of sorts. And if a little homemade jelly was left in a jar, it was a delight.

"Isn't God good in providing us with a nice warm home and good bread?" Mom would ask, expecting a positive response.

Our heads would nod, and Grace and I would stuff the tea-soaked bread into our hungry mouths.

Before we went to our beds, my mother might once more remind me of King David's statement: "I was young and now I am old, yet I have never seen the righteous or their children begging bread" (Psalm 37:25 NIV).

Well, I had seen Mom bake that bread, and we hadn't had to beg for it, so I felt certain that I was one of God's children. Even though some meat and potatoes would have made me feel a bit more blessed, it was a cheerful thought to go to bed on.

Well, many, many years have passed, and that old ramshackle house has long ago burnt to the ground. My darling mother is resting with the saints. Fortunately, today, I have much more than just plain baked bread and unsweetened tea to fill my belly.

"Time changes everything," Mom would say as she pointed to those words on a wall somewhere in that old house. And indeed, it has.

The years have flown by, but those dear old sayings still spring up today like a fountain in my soul when struggles and pain are my experiences. The example in living that my mother's life provided for her young daughter are ones that I try to keep alive for our future generations. I've spent a good portion of my days encouraging others to feel some of the hope and inspiration I was provided as a child.

When I speak to folks today about their cares or problems, they might not realize that the message or lessons I'm sharing are elaborations on some of those wonderful old sayings that inspired me in my youth.

Thanks, Mother, for all those life lessons you hung on our walls. Your dimes for their purchase weren't wasted.

# 9
# *Looking at Lilacs*

We lived in an old, dilapidated two-story wood-frame farmhouse that my grandfather had left to my mother. It was heated by a large wood- and coal-burning potbelly stove, which sat at the bottom of the stairs on the first floor of the house. At night, to save on our wood supply, Mom would turn down the airflow to the fire by partially closing the vents on the chimney pipe and the ones at the bottom of the stove so the fire would burn slower and not go out. She would open the vents in the morning to get a fire going again from the remaining coals. A kettle was usually kept on the top of the stove with hot water to use for tea if we had any or just some warm water if we didn't.

The house sat a little way from the blacktop road, down a bumpy lane through the woods. Sometime in the past, about five acres had been cleared for a field on which to farm.

Early in the morning hours, my dad would begin his match with the earth. He would hook our horse, Sis, up to his single plowshare and furrow the ground, just as men have done from all ages past. Then, up and down its lengths, he would scatter the winter's accumulation of manure, cleaned out from Sis's little barn each day and tossed onto a pile outside her barn door. Finally, the seeds or plant settings would go into the soil. A long and backbreaking chore, as one by one, we counted out the precious seeds and dropped them into the prepared holes or carefully set the small, delicate plants in place.

We carried buckets up and down the rows and poured a ladleful of water over each one of the few piles of seeds or young plants we had placed in the ground. Then we firmly piled the soil around it and patted it down.

Dad generally put in corn for feeding the horse and poultry and then perhaps some tomato and strawberry plants. My mother often had a jar of watermelon seeds saved from the prior year's crop. Sometimes we would have some pole beans that a neighbor was willing to share.

Around the perimeter of the field, my grandfather had planted some apple, cherry, peach, and pear trees. The blackberries and blueberries grew wild.

All the fruit and produce was gathered by all of us by summer's end and prepared by my mom to help us make it through the winter. Everything seemed to be about making it through winter, I suppose, because the winters were so hard to get through.

If we hadn't cut, stacked, and covered enough wood in the fall for burning in the stove during the winter, we would have to fight the snow and cold and go out into the woods where we would try to find some fallen trees that we could drag home, cut up, cover with the tarp, and *hope* it would be dry by the time we needed it.

I recall lying in that cold twin bed I shared with my sister, Grace, with bricks under our feet we had warmed on the stove, listening to the sound of the wind as it howled through the many cracks and holes in the walls of our upstairs bedroom. I can still see the pieces of cardboard that were often the only repair for a broken window.

The house had no electricity, and our water was pumped from the well outside—except when the pump froze up or went dry in the summer, which it often did. When things went wrong, on top of her many other challenges, my mother would say that the devil seemed to "work a lot of overtime" with us. There was no indoor plumbing or bathroom fixtures— or anything else, for that matter, that made life easy or comfortable.

During those freezing winter nights, an old galvanized metal bucket became the toilet for our household at night. This bucket, which was kept covered between uses by a lid that came with it, had to be toted downstairs each morning, carried out into the field, and emptied. It was then rinsed with a disinfectant called Creolin and then carried back upstairs with us at night. My sister and I took turns with that most unpleasant chore, and when doing it, we were, of course, very careful.

In the daylight hours, for our "constitutional requirements" (and just as equally demeaning to my young life) there stood about sixty feet from our back door an ancient outhouse, now formed of aged gray wood. Leaning foolishly, it seemed to mock my longing to escape the images that surrounded me. How I hated that ugly little shack.

Now, there was an "upkeep" procedure that Mom employed every few months to the outhouse. She would get a bag of lime and pour some down each of the two toilet holes. Country folks referred to that as "sweetening" the reception area under the outhouse. It seems the lime worked to speed up the organic process of nature and break down the matter so the ground beneath it all would absorb it better.

There were cracks in the aged wood of the door of that outhouse. You could peer through the cracks and tell when anyone else was heading down the path in your direction and call out to let them know it was occupied.

That outhouse only took up a four-by-four piece of earth on this planet, yet it spread over a big piece of my soul for a long time. Looking back, I now know that there was a life message waiting for me to eventually discover that has helped to shape my thinking. You see, from the many years of continuous use of that old outhouse, the ground surrounding it had become exceptionally fertile, and then, miraculously it now seems, up from this ground grew a lilac tree. And not just any old lilac tree, but one that seemed to grow in leaps and bounds until it dwarfed the outhouse and its branches hung upon its roof.

Soon it was producing monstrous-sized clusters of deep purple flowers. Those flowers lasted and lasted. When the summer breeze passed over those flowers, you could smell them all over the farm. I was always disappointed when the last of the lilacs went. To this day, I have never seen or found a lilac tree to equal its beauty or fragrance. And I have looked. I smile to realize the reciprocity of the matter, in that, without the outhouse, the lilacs would not have existed in such largesse.

The lifelong lesson I gained from the lilacs and the outhouse has helped me find the proper perspective on life and its many situations. I found that if you stood in the back door of our old house and looked out toward the field, your view would be that of that broken-down old outhouse with all its ugly features and its humiliating reminders of your station in life. However, there was another point of view to be found if you sought it. If you were out in the field instead and looking toward the house, why, in that very same spot, all that you could see was lilacs! You couldn't even tell that old outhouse existed. The lilacs in all their beauty overwhelmed that place, and all sight of the ugliness was erased.

My life has been so full of pain, grief, and sorrow that my outlook at times has been ugly and bleak and uncomfortable to bear—sort of like what the sight of that old outhouse was to my youthful view. In those times, I have asked my soul, "Please show me the lilacs. Take my heart from this place where all I see and feel is hurtful and sad. Take my spirit to where I can see the flowers blooming from these trying circumstances. Inspire my mind to see things from another perspective: that of hope and trust and joy."

And it will happen that by trusting in That Power that made the lilacs grow up from the soil of rot and decay, a new view of things will soon take root and grow in my heart and mind. In time, the pain will be swallowed up by the beauty of life that finds its way to me again—like the fragrance of those lilacs on the summer air.

# 10
## A Country Kitchen Door

A voice, a voice is calling me from a country kitchen door.

In apron stained, she looks the same. I see her there once more.

Oh, vision sweet and lovely, please don't fade from view; because my heart is longing for your smile anew.

The jelly jars, the boiling pots—sweet odors from the yore …

I weep that she no longer stands in that country kitchen door.

Don't fade from view, dear mother. Let me smell the rising bread.

Again, we'll chat of this and that dancing through my head.

The tablecloth will look the same, the fireplace will burn.

I'll nestle in your lap once more …

Return, oh youth, return!

The days my place was empty, I regret with bitter tears.

Yet oft in dreams, like now, it seems,

Her voice still calms my fears.

# II

# *Summer Fields*

I have no problem recalling certain summers of my youth. Summers where I often walked along country roads with my niece and best friend, Dottie Belle, who lived nearby. We would walk and talk for miles.

If we came upon a field of tall summer wheat, we just couldn't resist the urge to play within its sweet-smelling acres. We would both know what we wanted to do there—what we had done so many times before. We would each let out a whoop and take off in different directions, ducking down here and there to see where the other one might appear and then finding the greatest amusement in discovering how close or how far away from each other we might find ourselves.

It may seem silly to today's youth who have so much to fill their days and countless opportunities for pleasure and entertainment, yet she and I have some of our happiest memories revisiting those special days when nature was our game board and silliness was our goal.

We were little girls living in a place of safety. That in itself is hard to find today. We enjoyed a spot on earth where danger wasn't around every corner. We were free to wander and imagine and respond to whatever the season offered in its youthful promptings to play.

Life was filled with silly things for the two of us to enjoy together, and I'm grateful for those sweet moments that eased the other kind.

To this day, decades later, I never come upon a field of wheat or corn without wanting to get out of the car and run and play there once again.

And so, I ask you, "How many games remain within our memories with the potential to rise up over the years and thrill us all over again?"

# 12
## A Thought

Without dreams, the soul perishes.
But with them, our spirit is ageless.

# 13
# My Father's Grave

I had ridden around St. Mary's Cemetery a dozen times since my dad passed away but was never able to find the stone that marked his grave. When I was younger, I didn't know that there were people you could ask about these things. Then, as I got older, I got caught up in the affairs of my own life and family and rarely thought of it. When I did, I would just go there and walk around where I vaguely thought it should be, but I never could find it. Mom was dead. My older sister, Grace, lived in another state and didn't go to cemeteries.

Now after some ten or more years, for some reason, I had impulsively gone there again. This time, I was fifty-eight years old. I had just fought a battle with breast cancer, and I didn't feel like getting out and walking all over the place. I was slowly driving down the cemetery roads and looking around like a hand was going to reach out and wave to me and say, "Hey, Sis," as dad used to call me, "over here."

I'm not sure what lured me there. It just seemed important that I locate him while I was still living in this area. I was only ten years old when he died, but I remember it all very well.

He had come home from Jefferson Hospital in Philadelphia that day. The county health nurse had taken him up there. He had throat cancer and had been having trouble breathing. He told my mother, as I listened on, that they had tried to remove some of the tumor that was slowly strangling him. Because he was so weak and short of wind, they hadn't

Leona Flowers

wanted to anesthetize him. That was 1950, and they didn't know too much about dealing with cancer back then.

I remember feeling so sorry for him and asking, "Did it hurt, Daddy?"

His eyes were loving and looked weary as he smiled that thin smile of his. "Nah, it just tickled a little." Then he asked if I wanted to follow him upstairs to the bed and take his shoes off for him.

It was July 17 and very hot. I took his hand, and it seemed like I pulled him upward a little as we made our way to the bedroom.

I loved my dad. My mother was the one to depend on, but my dad was the one who made me laugh and taught me songs and told me wonderful stories.

"Will you be all right?" I asked as I dropped the last shoe on the floor next to the bed.

He rubbed my head. "Right as rain," he mustered. "Now you go on down and play. I'll talk to you when I get up."

With that assurance, I went downstairs.

Strangely, Mom told me that I could go on down the road to play for a while at my sister Viola's house with her daughter, Dottie Belle. Poor and with little time for play, I raced off before she changed her mind. Dottie Belle and I happily spent the afternoon playing paper dolls on her bedroom floor.

I can't recall, having lost myself in the little girl world of imagination, how long that I spent there before Grace came breathlessly into the room to tell me that Mom wanted me home. *Right away.*

Without explanation from Grace and, stranger still, without me asking anything, we raced down the road toward home.

Halfway down the lane that led back to our house, I spotted Mom walking quickly toward us. When she was within our hearing range, she cried out, "Sis, your daddy is dead. He's gone … he's gone … he's gone. Oh, God, what are we going to do without him?"

By this time, she had her arms around me, and my young brain was reeling. I broke free and began running for the house so that I could race up the stairs and wake up my daddy to show her that she had made a terrible mistake and show her that he was only sleeping just like he had told me he was going to do. He would open his eyes and then laugh and tell me that he had just been fooling Mommy. I needed so badly to see his face.

But Mom caught up to me and told me that my daddy wasn't there—not in the house, not in the bed where he had patted me on the head and told me to go play, and not anywhere on the farm. He was gone. Mom said that he had been taken into town by the undertaker.

For a child, losing a parent is like a hurricane hitting their psyche. I felt deceived. I felt like Mom had known that he was going to die and still sent me away. Now, he was at some strange place that I knew nothing about, and I had lost the last chance to ever speak to him again. I needed my daddy to hold me as I cried.

There were three days of viewing for my dad, and then his coffin was taken to St. Mary's, the church where Dad would go each morning for early Mass before starting out on the streets with his load of produce or whatever he would be selling off the back of his horse and wagon.

The funeral Mass was the first time I had been in a Catholic church. Dad had let Mom raise us as Protestants. Sitting there, unable to understand everything that was going on, like when to sit and when to kneel, I wished he had brought me there with him when he was still alive instead of having to go there for the first time with his coffin.

I remember weeping and weeping through it all like I was in some strange nightmare that I couldn't wake up from. I needed my daddy to comfort me in his warm, friendly arms. The one I needed was the one who was gone. In the funeral home, I kept staring at the part of his face that I could see over the sides of the coffin and felt like he might suddenly sit up at any moment and say with that Irish humor of his, "Boy, I'm sure glad to see all of you. I just did this to get all of you to come and visit me." But he never did.

It was that wonderful lighthearted personality of my dad's—as opposed to my mother's very serious nature—that had helped keep some balance in my young life amid all the grueling poverty.

In the weeks, months, and years that followed his death, I would think and rethink about his final year and of how terribly deprived, yet uncomplaining my wonderful father was.

Two incidents especially stand out in my mind. Both took place within months of his death. One happened the previous winter, and the other occurred just days before he died.

When I think about how cold it was that winter of 1949, I still get a chill.

My parents would spend days using our old horse to pull fallen trees out of the woods. For hours, with a long two-man saw, they would cut the trees into stove-sized logs that they would load onto the back of the wagon. With the wood stacked high, my dad would drive the wagon the five miles into town and go up and down the streets to find customers for the wood.

Sometimes, it would be rich people in big brick houses with fireplaces in the parlors or maybe poor people like ourselves who couldn't afford coal for their stoves. No matter how long it took, my dad would eventually find someone who wanted his load of wood.

Five dollars for the whole load. Five dollars for days of hard work. Just enough to get some bread, coffee, a few cans of milk, white flour, a couple of soup bones, potatoes, onions, lard, salt, a mess of greens, and a couple of bars of laundry soap. Staples. Just some basics to help us survive the hard days of winter without asking charity of anyone.

Anyway, on one of those kinds of days, my dad surprised and delighted me by asking me if I wanted to go with him and his load of wood into town. I was always happiest when I was with my dad. After I jumped in the wagon, we headed down the country road toward town.

Mother had bundled me up as best she could with newspapers in my boots and a couple thick pair of socks on my hands, but I was still cold.

"Jump down and walk," Dad said. "You'll be warmer."

He was walking in front of the horse and blowing into his red and cracked ungloved hands. He would occasionally stomp his feet as he walked down the road to "keep the blood moving." I became aware that I had boots on, and he didn't.

We went through a wooded area known to the locals as the "Muttontown Woods." There was an old dump pile there set back from the road a few feet where people would go and throw trash that they didn't feel like toting to the regular township dump or didn't want to accumulate on their own properties.

Whatever the reasons for that dump's existence, on that day, my dad was glad it was there because sitting right up there near the top, covered with some of the falling snow, was an old pair of black, buckle-up rubber boots! Sighting them, Dad brought the horse to a sudden halt and scrambled off over the branches and garbage to get to the treasure he saw waiting for him. After hitting them vigorously against the trees to get the snow off, he hurriedly made his way back and climbed up into the wagon.

"Boy, the Lord sure was looking out for your old dad today, wasn't he, Sis?" he said with a smile and a wink.

I nodded, happy to see him with the boots on his feet. I was hoping that maybe God might have stuck some gloves down inside those old black boots too, but there weren't any gloves there. I guess God figured the boots were about as much help as my dad needed that day. I guess they were. My dad was grateful with his find and wore them all winter long.

He sold the load of wood before dark, went to the A&P store on the way home, and shopped for the groceries Mom had written on the list.

I have never been able to forget how happy my dad was on that cold winter day so long ago just to get an old pair of cast-off black rubber boots.

Then, in the days before he died that hot summer of 1950, when he was only fifty-five, I did something that still makes me feel guilty.

My dad's battle with throat cancer had become difficult, and he hadn't been able to help support the family for several months. Mom had to take what she called "handouts" from some of her family in the form of food or a few dollars. It was hard for her to do, but she had the burden of my dad's illness, with doctor visits and all, so she swallowed her pride and took some help. But just as little as she could, promising that, when she got on her feet, she would pay each one of them back. She knew they were all poor as well.

Money was tight, but the one "luxury" item mom allowed for was some 7-Up soda for my dad because he had such difficulty swallowing. He enjoyed the 7-Up, and it seemed to be something that went down easier.

In those days, they used to bottle it in little seven-ounce bottles. I suppose that's where the name came from. They were very small bottles. So when he would ask for some of it, we would chip some ice from the block of ice in the icebox, put the ice in a small saucepan, pour the 7-Up over the ice, and carry it to him.

One day, he had made his way down to the apple orchard and was resting against one of the trees. Mom had been offered some work in someone's field and had taken Grace with her. She had left me home to care for my dad. I went to the orchard where he was sitting to see if there was anything he wanted me to do for him.

His once delightful voice was raspy as he asked me if I would please fix him some soda. I ran back to the house, chipped off the ice, and filled the saucepan with it. I lifted off the lid from that wonderful, fizzy, sweet-smelling, clear 7-Up and poured it over the ice.

The saucepan got that sweat all over the outside, and in that sizzling month of July, the sight of that cold saucepan of 7-Up was just too tempting for a sweltering ten-year-old. I brought the saucepan to my lips and took a sip. Aware of how little soda was in that small bottle and how sick my poor Dad was, I instantly felt guilty.

I carried the saucepan to him there in the orchard, and he lovingly asked me if I wanted to take a drink. I shook my head, sure that he could tell that some of it was missing. But he only smiled, thanked me, and told me that I could go play if I wanted to—and that I didn't need to stay there with him.

I walked away, disliking myself for my act and thinking that God must not be very happy with a kid who would drink some of her father's 7-Up when it was so hot, and he was so sick. I could buy tons of 7-Up today, but I don't.

As I was driving around St. Mary's Cemetery, I thought, *The landscape keeps changing around here. Houses have been torn down. A new parkway passes by the cemetery now. It doesn't even look like it did the last time I was out here looking for his grave. Why do I think I might find it now?*

When I had gone there in 1950, I had been in the undertaker's car with my mom and Grace. My parents never learned to drive motor vehicles. If they needed to go somewhere that required travel by auto, they had to depend on someone else to take them. In the cemetery that day, I was driving a lovely ruby-colored Cadillac Eldorado.

As my mother always used to say, "Time changes everything." And indeed, it had! I had determined that time *would* change everything for me! I made a vow to myself after my father's death that I would not die as poor as he did. The memories of his life and his death were a motivating force in my life.

I was just about ready to call it a day when something strong inside my mind suddenly told me to stop the car. I did. I put the car in park, left the motor running, and followed my urge to get out of the car at that very place and walk a few steps. As I did, I looked down at the ground—and an inch below the grass level was my dad's gravestone: James Joseph Dean 1895–1950.

I was stunned to have found him, just like that, and I knew that I had been led there by some strange force that wanted me to know where he was.

"Well, hell, Dad," I said as tears started forming from my eyes. I stooped down and lovingly brushed my hand across the surface of the stone. "It looks like I got here just in time. It wouldn't have been long before the grass grew over this, and I would have probably never found you."

I happily cleared it as best I could.

Perhaps it was just the overwhelming emotions of the experience and my longing to be near him once more, but I imagined his hand on my shoulder and sensed that he was near me in that place and in that moment, smiling in that old sweet way. I closed my eyes and let it all wash over me. "I still miss and love you, Dad," I whispered.

I don't know how long I kneeled there touching my father's name on the headstone. I only know I didn't want that long-sought connection to be broken.

When I finally stood, I had to suck in a breath to keep from falling! A grateful smile slowly calmed me, and I walked back to the car with his wonderful voice in my ear. I felt stronger for having gone there. His beautiful spirit was comforting me in the same way he comforted and brightened my days so long ago.

I looked heavenward and couldn't help but breathe a little prayer for having been led here that day. I knew it was a gift to my spirit and that it would allow me to finally forgive the child who took that sip of 7-Up from his cup so many years ago. *Perhaps now I can let go of that hurt and shame and remember only the joy of my father's love for me.*

Say what you will about these things, but I truly feel a kindly angel led me back to my father's grave and the peace for which my soul had long awaited.

Leona with her father in 1948

# 14
# Stories in the Night

Papa, tell me stories as you did so long ago,
Lift me now upon your lap in the lantern's glow,
Let me feel the thrill again at wonders yet unseen,
Far from present labors to when the fields were green.
Let me look into your face and see you smile again,
Feel your hand upon my cheek,
Then kiss away my pain.
Oh, the love I knew there safe in Papa's arms,
Peace as with no other.
Safe from all life's harms,
Oft' at eve I hear him,
Soft words against my ears.
Papa, tell me stories,
Tonight, turn back the years.

# 15
# On Being Kind

In 1965, a pregnant young woman about my age came to my door selling paper roses. I had just spent my last two dollars on formula for my own baby, and sadly, I had nothing with which to buy her flowers. Instead, I told her I was just sitting down for lunch and asked if she'd like to join me for a cup of tea and a sandwich. She eagerly took me up on my offer. That day began a friendship between us that lasted for forty-five years until her death from breast cancer in 2010.

The child my friend gave birth to was a little girl who chose from the time she was a toddler to be a near me as often as she could and be a part of my life. And as she grew, she wanted my input on every life decision she had to consider. Over the years, she spent countless days in my home with my family and me. I would not have wanted to have experienced life without her warm and wonderful presence in it.

Her mother took great pleasure in her daughter and my special relationship. I've been happy being "Auntie" to that little girl who is now a beautiful, gracious woman.

My mind has returned often to the decision I made that day when I offered to share a meal with a stranger. I think about how I might have made a different choice and turned away one who became a lifelong friend. I realize that by making a simple response of kindness—even though I couldn't make a purchase from her—I have gained so much. What a loss to my life it would have been if I had just said, "I'm sorry" and closed the door to her.

But I didn't—and that choice has made all the difference.

How could I have known that the simple act of sharing a cup of tea and a sandwich could have opened the door to such a return of karmic blessing?

My mother often said that it costs us very little to be kind. For me, it was just a cup of tea and a sandwich. What a beautiful bargain it was for me that day.

# 16
## Mother Said

My mother used to say that people can become better-looking to you as you observe the kindness and pleasantness they have within them.

However, she also informed me that they can grow ugly to you and lose whatever beauty you may have seen in them at first as they begin to reveal their mean or rude nature.

# 17
# The Blessings of Nature

I grew up in the country. I've always been grateful for having my start where I was living close to nature and surrounded by the things God made and not the things people made. I climbed trees, wandered through woods, ate fruit right off the bushes and trees, and had animals as playmates.

There's something wonderful and pure about lying on piles of warm leaves in the fall and peering up at a clear blue sky through the brightly colored trees. You weave your dreams there—and then perhaps doze off from the sheer sensual pleasure of it all. This tent of creation that fed my spirit and mind was compensation, I now realize, for the material things I lacked in a harsh and deprived childhood.

The memories of the woodlands and fields of golden corn, of wading in clear streams of water, of swimming in lakes in quiet early mornings, of hearing the songs of the birds from your window, and gathering wildflowers along a country road are pleasures that stay with you for a lifetime. They also contribute to good health.

By breathing in fresh air, we are invigorated. It is an established fact that certain fragrances bring about positive chemical changes within our cells. Thus, by taking in the simple remedies that nature provides for us, our dynamic balance can be restored, our sagging spirits can be enlivened, our intellects can be stimulated, and our moods can be brightened.

Leona Flowers

I can recall the occasions over the years when I've gone on long hikes. Under the influence of the natural world's uplifting beauty, I was changed from how I had felt just the day before. When my eyes would rest on the awesome landscapes that continually lay before and around me, my body seemed infused with energy and light.

I read once that there is something about gazing at distant horizons, either on land or sea, that brings about an opening up or expansion of the powers of the functions of the mind. So you can see how living in an environment of buildings all around you might be ruinous to your creativity—or at least stint what it might be able to do under different circumstances. This makes one understand why geniuses, like Thoreau, might seek out the pleasant surroundings of the countryside.

Many artists have found inspiration in the quiet power of the natural world; beautiful flowers, roaring seas, vast hills, and valleys are all conducive to opening the portals of our creative selves and releasing the inner gifts waiting there.

So, as one who has planted and harvested and wandered and played amidst lovely spaces, I urge you, when you find yourself despondent or burdened with care, go out into nature. When you want your eyes to rest on things that are pure and restorative and escape the destructive and the ugly, go into nature. When your heart informs you that you need to hear the songs of birds instead of all the wearing sounds that invade your head through your ears, go into nature.

One scientist said we are suffering from eye and ear pollution. Creation holds the cure for many of our modern ills. So, take a plane, a train, a car, or a bicycle, and go in search of nature's healing agents. An old song declares that the "best things in life are free," and perhaps they are, but even if it costs a bit to help you find your way to where nature's doctors dwell, it will still be far less costly than the illnesses that can arise from never going there.

Renewal, peace, inspiration, and health are all waiting for you in some pleasant place, and Nature's voice deep within you calls you there.

# 18
# *Destiny*

The only person you are destined to be is the person you decide to be.
—Ralph Waldo Emerson

# 19
## Mother Said

My mother used to say, "You can't just sit around and feel sorry for yourself because indulged for very long, you'll soon find you won't be able to do anything other than just sit around." She believed in the power of purpose.

I can recall instances of being down in bed with an ailment of some kind and receiving a call from my mother. She would encourage me to "get up and do something just as early as you're able—and you'll be feeling better sooner."

I used to think she didn't realize how sick I was or the degree of discomfort I was experiencing, but the years have shown me that she was right. When I have focused on getting myself up on my feet and doing something that needed to be done, I have discovered more often than not that I did regain my strength more quickly than when I allowed myself to give in to the problem.

"Mind over matter," she would say. I realized over the years that she was onto something. It is probably that philosophy of hers that has helped me to finally get this book produced. Thanks again, Mother.

# 20
# Some Things Are Up to You

Life is all about perspective. We can look at it from any angle *we* choose. Perhaps we'll choose to live our lives with a well-directed heart and a mind that functions as wide and inclusive—or we'll have a view of people and situations that's so narrow we're incapable of ever glimpsing the larger picture.

We can count money or seek to count the stars. We can shrink our hearts to love only ourselves or embrace life and everything in it. We can spend our lives waiting for the right moment to come along or plant ourselves boldly into *every* moment and not let many pass away uninfused with a beneficial thought or act from us.

I think we will find life to be an easier road to travel if we see the world as accepting us and loving us and welcoming all that we have to bring into it. I believe it aids us to have a vision where we see ourselves as *purposed* and meaningful in this life we've been given. With that type of outlook, we can live our lives happily and dynamically!

# 21

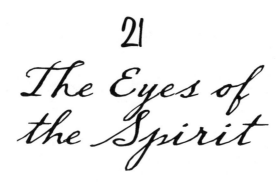

## The Eyes of the Spirit

Mark 8:18 (NIV) says, "Do you have eyes but fail to see, and ears but fail to hear?"

It seems to me that these words speak to us about the lack of vision that exists among us and of the internal voice to which we will not listen.

Its intent is not as an insult, but as a warning. It is urging us to note our lack of preparedness for things that may come upon us with which we've never dealt.

It speaks of a disability of the spirit that may cause us to be unable to grasp the greater lessons intended for our welfare when we require an understanding of reality beyond what the material world presents to our senses.

This seeing and hearing of the soul is a gift that heaven offers, but which we must seek. Without its aid, we may slip and fall into a crippling silence of the spirit.

# 22
# The Dynamics of Choices and Change

"Pick a door!" the TV hosts shouts to the trembling contestant on a game show. "Pick a door—and let's see what prize is waiting for you behind it."

There may have been some anxiety related to making the most profitable choice, but all in all, it's not really a tough one.

There are some truths about making choices that we need to see and understand. In my younger years, I had a good pastor friend who impressed upon my mind the power that lies within every person's choices to affect their own lives *and* the lives of others. Therefore, we have an obligation to consider the dynamics and possible outcomes of the choices we make.

First, let me note that when we make a choice, we're actually making *two* choices simultaneously because when we choose to do *one* thing, we are also choosing *not* to do another. For example, if I choose to not take a job right now and go to college instead, I have chosen to get an education with the prospect of a well-paying job when I graduate, and I have also chosen to forgo the money and fun I could be enjoying in that very same time. I could also choose to take a low-paying job now and be making some money, but then I have sacrificed or postponed the education that could lead to greater rewards for me later. Both possibilities have benefits, and both have costs, so it's important to weigh both options carefully and strategically.

You might think of some of life's circumstances as a giant game of chess. If your goal is to win, then you shouldn't rush to make your move. Instead, you should study the board while anticipating the possibilities your choice will make available to your opponent when it becomes *their* turn to make their choice. It's important to recognize that once you've made your move, your decision has ended. You have no control whatsoever on the actions your opponent might then make in response. So, you can see how your choice of action needs to be reasonably well constructed in your mind before proceeding.

In the game of life, as in chess, you shouldn't proceed with taking actions until you are certain that you've considered all the potential outcomes to your move and feel a certain level of comfort that you have chosen the best of the options that were *available to you*. Then, fortify yourself to be prepared to accept the outcome.

We each want to be winners in life as often as we can. We want to make the decisions that bring us to a happy, healthy, balanced, and abundant manner of living. So understanding the dynamics of choice is important in every aspect of living.

All of us at one time or another allow other people or circumstances to provoke us into acting in ways that are not beneficial to a good long-term outcome for ourselves. Submitting to a not-well-considered impulse may provide some temporary satisfaction, but in the long term, regret is often what we reap.

As often as possible, our words and actions should be under our control. It takes discipline and may be quite challenging at times, but it pays off in the long run. It may even give you an advantage in your dealings with others. After all, life is mostly about engaging with other free agents who are also rightfully exercising *their* own free choices.

On January 19, 2013, Elaine Shpungin, PhD, wrote an article in *Psychology Today*. She wrote, "It turns out that what you watch, read, listen to and play can affect your mood, temper, and even how kind and generous you are afterward!" Whatever attracts and holds our attention has a great deal to do with making us react the way we do in our choices and actions. These things empower and enlighten us over our lifetime—or diminish and weaken our ability to choose rightly.

Now, in addressing our relationship to change, I've found that one of the biggest factors standing in the way of self-growth is unwillingness to change, adapt to change, or adapt to new behaviors. It's a documented fact that many people are afraid of change. We cling to sameness with a kind of belief that there's some mental or emotional "safeness" in doing so.

It seems odd to me—as I consider time, space, matter, and energy—that something we humans resist so strongly, *change*, is the one great constant of the vast universe. Being stuck in one mind-set can be a hindrance to growth and a more expansive vision of life.

How can I best share my conclusions that if we want to grow a greater awareness, become new and wiser human beings, and discover ourselves and the world we live in, we must be prepared to change the way we think, the choices we make, and our actions or inaction.

For someone like me who mines life for every gift, even those that may temporarily be hidden, believes in the great possibilities in our existence, and searches for every avenue of upward growth, I've never understood why a person wouldn't—or couldn't—see how changing their thoughts, actions, choices, perspectives, and philosophies could improve their lives.

The human mind awes me with its capacity to adapt, overcome, and discover resolutions to the problems the Creative Power has programmed into humanity. It is intended to move us continually forward as we confront different circumstances and evolve with them.

We are given insights into our skills and strengths as we confront each new challenge of being human and understanding the purposes behind surviving and living to maturity as we were intended. Our instincts and intuition provide guidance for where we need to go to gather the strengths we require and how best to apply the skills and strengths we already have.

I've experienced so many changes in my own life, starting with my earliest memory. The choices that life has afforded me have often been very few. So I chose to accept the challenge that I would either discover how to adapt to or overcome the tough circumstances of my existence—or break under the struggle. I chose not to be broken.

I chose to change what—and when—I needed to change and was determined to find the means to rise each time my flesh or spirit fell from the ordeal. I do not pose the premise that it's easy, but it is a choice and one that I often knew my survival depended upon. After many years of choices and changes, I have concluded that our struggles of mind, heart,

Leona Flowers

and spirit are won or lost upon the battlefield of our will and within the seedbeds of our choices.

I've been the recipient of the love and urgings of many dear people who, when observing my pain or disability, prayed for me to rise again and find my footing going forward once more. And I always have. Yet the courage, reasoning, and adaptability necessary to engage the challenges we face each day must be drawn from the storehouses of our own souls. Fill it with a philosophy that fuels your determination to adapt and change as often as necessary to make you the owner of this life that was given to you.

In my own reflections on creation, I find it to be a wonderful thing that I would miraculously come into being in endless time and space. I am so continually thrilled at my own existence that I consider any struggles I meet as a small payment for this awesome privilege. So, I am willing to be changed by the forces of life and circumstances if that is heaven's plan for me, and I will strive to make better and more beneficial choices and changes as long as life and time will allow me.

Choice and change are the two oars that move us over the sea of life.

# 23
# How Divine

Despite how you fancy in your mind that you have an understanding of the Mind that created the universe and placed the planets in their places and designed your DNA, pardon me if I say I just don't think that's possible. And I don't think it's anything we should struggle with.

I think we've been given ample enough mini lessons in the natural world and our own physical bodies to provide tremendous insights which are intended by that Mind to bring us connections—if we seek them.

There can be epiphanies if we trust that our Creator-Parent wants to help us be at peace with things that are unknowable. Consider the newborn baby boy who doesn't have an inkling of knowledge of the mother who has forced him out of her womb and into this plane of existence. This newly existent being cannot comprehend the complexity of this one who feeds him from her laden breasts, a custom-designed product from nature to perfectly suit the unique chemistry of his cells. This small, helpless, speechless, and vulnerable human being doesn't have to make pleas, pledges, or promises in order for her to rock him to sleep with the beat of her heart or comfort and protect him and keep him well. And she will do all this as he wails and flails. He will not anger or annoy her in his ignorance. He cannot grasp the concept that because she gave him life and she is his parent she will watch over him and guide his attempts at surviving and understanding life.

This being who he will call "Mother" will be near him every step of the way as he moves along the path on his own journey of discovery. He did not have to understand her. He did not have to fear her magnificent life-sustaining presence. In his limited stages of development, before he could look out over life and find out what his place was in it, he didn't have to know her mind or the measure of her wisdom and her power—or her plans for him. She created him, and she loved him.

He only had to look up to her, trust her, and smile.

# 24

# There's A Lot to Be Learned—If We'll Learn It

I recently viewed a video on human conception that revealed the development of the fetus in the womb and the process of birth. I was so awed by what I was seeing taking place before my eyes that I watched it again with my husband. We thrilled at it together. Watching a human life start to exist was so miraculous that it brought me emotionally close to tears.

I watched another video where a flower went from seed to full blossom in slow motion. It was another glorious experience. It was intoxicating in the wonder of it all.

I am one who finds a great sermon in the magnificent potential of an acorn and have spent many happy hours contemplating the inexplicable wonders of nature in its mysterious and awesome activity. I've also been moved by the marvelous revelations in the life of a caterpillar! I watched a nature program where a caterpillar created his cocoon—grave clothing of sorts—from his own body. Later, he pushed until he broke open that thing that had entombed him for days or weeks while a transformation or metamorphosis was taking place.

When he emerged, he was no longer a dark, ugly caterpillar. He had become a beautiful new creature that arose on glorious wings. This caterpillar-turned-butterfly would thereafter live an entirely different kind of existence than what he had lived up until that moment. He would no longer crawl among other insects amid the dirt on the ground. He was reincarnated, and he could rise upward on gossamer wings toward the sky. He could set lightly upon flowers and dine upon their nectar.

Nature had resurrected the humble caterpillar, but the inherent capacity, the possibility, had actually been within him all along! To my seeking mind, the power and plans of nature revealed through this simple example, through the transformation of this most humble of all creatures, is a message to us if we'll allow it to be. To my studious mind, it was an epiphany. It was a reason for our own human hope.

As I've allowed myself to be so inspired, it seems obvious to me that as we evolve through time, our intended way will always be upward, like the caterpillar to the butterfly—to some more glorious plane of existence—and not backward or downward to the dirt and the bug.

These kinds of messages are all around if we'll but see them. However, they require our choosing to often take our focus off of the useless and vain and turn it instead to the voices of nature in a world whose very makeup is a study in awe and wonder.

Folks say they long for proof that we are not alone in this world, yet the messages we have been given appear to go unobserved for the most part. My wish is that everyone will be as awed and comforted by the manifestations within nature as I have been.

I personally believe that I was led to observe so many things of this sort in order to be of a surety that any wisdom or soundness of thought that I might hope to gain during my life will be dependent on my continuing to trust the Author and the Creator of all things. And that I should continue to rely on *that Mind* wherein power, purpose, and design reside.

Finally, similarly to that ugly little caterpillar I mentioned, I believe that I too shall soon hear a call for change. And *I* shall be the one dressed in grave clothing, awaiting my own mysterious miracle of flight. Because life here in this world has been so filled with lessons and revelations that you can be certain I believe wings of some sort are waiting for me.

Nature teaches me all I need to consider in order to remain believing that there is a Presence at work behind the curtain of life.

# 25
## The Lesson of the Puddles

Those who won't be ruled by the rudder must be ruled by the rock. When I was a kid, my family was living out on the farm in Alloway, New Jersey. The house sat back from Kerlin Road, down a long dirt lane. I will never forget that lane. How could I have ever known how that bumpy old piece of earth was going to teach me a life lesson in better judgment? We had no money to surface the lane or even pay for dirt to fill in all its deep ruts. So, over time, those many ruts got even worse from the cars and trucks that regularly drove in and out. When it rained heavily, the lane became a series of mud puddles.

I walked up and down that lane every day to catch the school bus or get the mail or whatever else took me out to the blacktop road. During long dry spells, there was absolutely nothing of concern for me related to the lane or its many ruts. But when it rained? Ahh! Now we have the makings of my tale.

For the most part, when those ruts turned into mud puddles, I could still come tearing down that lane—day or night—and leap over every one of them without a splash. Since I knew where the ruts were, I knew where the mud puddles would be. They were sort of laid out like a map in my young brain.

However, when the ground was still soft from a rain, someone's vehicle might get stuck. All the churning to get free would gouge out a new puddle. A new layout in my head was necessary, but it didn't always happen.

I recall vividly the result of those lapses in my mental preparedness, those uncomfortable times when I hadn't adjusted my calculations for a new puddle. On those tragic occasions when I would be racing homeward down the lane some dark night, I would find myself misjudging the distances between the puddles. Suddenly, I would be splashed from head to toe—drenched with dark, ugly water and lots of mud! The rest of my trip to the house was unbearable for me. I had nothing to wipe the mud off my face, and I was sloshing in my shoes. Some grit from the mud might be in my eyes, and my dress would be hanging as a soggy mess. I had to call to my mother outside our door to come help me since I couldn't enter the house in my terribly wet, dripping condition. And if it was cold, I was probably crying as well. So, I'll tell you, it didn't take many missteps like that to fix in my mind the need to calculate my movements and stay on top of changes in the terrain over which I had to travel if I was to avoid unpleasant happenings in the future.

I often draw upon the lessons I learned from those experiences I had so long ago when I'm dealing with current mud puddles—the messes I get myself into by not seeing the need to change my tactics when the need to do so presents itself. If I've been doing things in a certain way that is "muddying" up my life, I know I need to make adjustments to my thoughts and actions. I need to stop making assumptions about things or people that no longer apply and see the need to get my head around things the way they are occurring in the here and now. I need to pay close attention to my environment and regularly update the map in my head to avoid mistakes in my judgement that will leave me now, as it did then, in uncomfortable and messy places.

# 26
# *The Way of Wisdom*

The *American College Dictionary* states that wisdom is "the knowledge of what is true or right, coupled with just judgment as to actions." In my estimation, this level of knowledge can only be earned through life experience, however hard or painful it may be at times.

When I was a child, I read the Bible a lot. I thought it was a book that had all the answers and all the secrets for how to deal with everything people might ever have to come up against in life. In the troubled and painful years of my childhood, I believe I was seeking promises that would give me hope and courage. My mother often sang an old hymn that asked, "Where can I go but to the Lord?" In times of need as great as ours, God was the only One to whom we could turn. Without that faith, I think we would have perished psychologically.

My mother's strong faith influenced me to believe that God would always keep his Word. So, the hope I found in his promises was exactly what a poor, fatherless little girl like me needed.

When I turned to its pages for help and direction, a lot of what was written in that old King James version of my mother's Bible was too hard for me to grasp. However, I was determined to grapple with its contents for the knowledge I knew was in there—waiting to be discovered by anyone who sought it. My Sunday school teacher admonished the class that when it came to knowing the will of God, to "seek and thou shalt find."

I began by reading the parts that were the simplest and easiest for me to understand, like the story of a Hebrew king named Solomon. When I got to the part about King Solomon and read that "God gave Solomon wisdom and very great insight, and a breadth of understanding as measureless as the sand on the seashore" (1 Kings 4:29 NIV), I was deeply affected. I read on with great interest. I wanted to know more about this quality God could give to his children called *wisdom.*

Next, I read essentially, that we should seek wisdom above all else: "For wisdom is more precious than rubies, and nothing you desire can compare with her" (Proverbs 8:11 NIV).

Nothing could compare to having wisdom? Nothing? Well, then, if wisdom was the very best thing to possess in life, then that was what *I* wanted because I was small and weak and had so little. I needed whatever heaven could provide to help lift me above those present circumstances. *Who wouldn't ask for wisdom if it says right there in God's Holy Word that it is the best thing to have in life?*

I was often alone on our farm after my father died. Mom had to work long hours in the can houses, preparing produce for products like ketchup, and she needed me to watch the house and care for the animals. One day, when I was there alone and reading the Bible about wisdom, my young mind decided that perhaps I should be bold enough to ask heaven if it would grant this wonderful power called wisdom to a kid like me. After all, a promise within the Bible implied that if you ask for something and you believed God doesn't change or lie, then—somewhat like in *Cinderella* or *The Wizard of Oz,* other favorite books of mine—he would grant your wish.

And so, with nothing to lose but life as it was for me, I slipped down to my knees, grasped my mother's Bible like a life raft, lay my head upon it, and began to pray. I don't remember everything I said in my prayer, but I do recall saying these words: "Please, Lord, please give me wisdom—and I don't care what it costs me!"

It's been many years since that long-ago day when I knelt before God with my youthful plea. The events that have followed and how I've faced them have written out the story of my life.

Did the prayer that I uttered hit the listening ear of God? And have the many struggles for light and understanding been the seeds of a gift that could only grow amid sorrow and loss? One thing I do know is that there is so much we *don't* know about life and its many mysteries.

Today, as I get closer to eighty, there are those who assure me in my hesitancy to lay claim to such a lofty quality as *wisdom* that I have accumulated a philosophy and approach to life that they associate with that term. Who knows? Perhaps my request was answered, and the prayer I uttered as a child hit its mark. Perhaps Providence measured me for the journey and has mapped out my experiences and circumstances ever since.

I consider the latter because, when looking back, I realize I was being led even when I was in great darkness of the soul amid the many times of sorrow and brokenness. I'll admit, with great honesty, that considering all the roads I've traveled and burdens my soul has endured since I knelt with my mother's Bible, I sometimes wonder if had I been shown how heavy a price one must pay for light and understanding—that I might not have chosen an easier path than the one that came with the wisdom I so coveted.

# 27
# The Aim of Kindness

If we're only kind to those who have been kind to us, and we are only generous to those who have been generous to us, then what have we accomplished? That is what the Good Book asks.

Surely, we should be kind to those whose own generosity of spirit has always been available to us. However, we should also be kind to those who are unable by their very circumstances to return to us anything other than gratitude. If praise was not our aim, then we received sufficient compensation with that humble response.

It's in this manner that we can take the better measure of our spirits, our true motivations, and our honesty with ourselves. It's a struggle we have always had—perhaps because we need feedback on whether we're being or becoming good people or not. I'm not sure.

If we are striving for higher ground for our struggling souls, then selflessness and humility are the ideal. I believe we should give because we are grateful that life has allowed us a bounty from which to give.

# 28
# Prayer Changes Things

The Good Book says, "The prayers of a righteous man (person) accomplishes much." Well, I'm one of those who believe in the power of rightly directed prayer.

Our son, Brian, has always been a most devoted son to me. When he was a toddler, if he saw me sit down, he would make his way to where I was, wrap his little arms around my legs, and rest his head upon my lap.

As a youngster, Brian would lie on the floor next to me if I was sick on the sofa—just in case I woke up and needed something. He always wanted to be there to hear and help me. As a teen, he wanted a metal detector for Christmas. With that detector in hand, he and I would happily go on "treasure hunts" together. We always talked and laughed together with a special mother-son bond.

During Brian's teen years, his spirituality grew along with his sense of personal duty to help others. He decided to attend a Christian academy with the intent of finding a place in life working as a youth counselor of some kind.

Brian was full of prolific ideas. His boundless confidence that things could be achieved delighted me. He was fearless and filled with an enthusiasm in everything he attempted.

Perhaps it was due to his youthful joie de vivre that he didn't exercise caution on that July day in 1977 when he visited a little North Jersey seaside town. I was later told that without ever having been there before—or having checked the depth of the water at the end of a long pier that he spied—my son ran out onto it and executed a beautiful swan dive into less than three feet of water.

Since that day, my son has never been able to walk with me or reach out his arms to embrace me or know life outside of a wheelchair. Brian has lived his life as a high-level quadriplegic.

After racing to the hospital that day, I had to make difficult decisions on the spot. For one, his spine was crushed. Portions of the shattered bone had severed nerves to most of his body, including nerves that affected the function of his lungs. They had to make a tracheotomy in his throat and connect him by hose to a respirator. As they sought to stabilize his spine, I had to decide whether they would try to insert a five-inch metal pin in his neck and reconstruct the bone around it or put a brace around his neck that he would have to live out his life in. I chose the metal pin.

After the neck reconstruction around the pin, they inserted metal bolts into the sides of his head and installed onto them a metal circular piece called a "halo." This halo had weights connected to it that served to pull on the head to take the pressure off the neck as the surgery healed.

Next, they strapped him—arms, chest, abdomen, and legs—to a device known as a Stryker frame (after the name of the manufacturer). His arms were straight out from his body, and they turned the frame at intervals to have him either facing the ceiling or the floor.

My child appeared to me, in this horrible position on the device with the halo bolted into his head, somewhat like the crucified Christ. It was almost unbearable for a mother. My heart and the hearts of all who loved Brian groaned at the sight of his suffering. During that horrible time, it seemed my eyes fought continually against the force of the tears that wanted to flow. Fear crushed our spirits because, without exception, not one of the many doctors who treated him offered us any measure of hope.

During the several weeks Brian was in that seaside hospital, he had one crisis after another.

One day, his vitals began slipping as he started hemorrhaging from his colon due to all the steroids that were being given him to fight infection. I was asked to step back from his side as several doctors rushed in and surrounded him. Blood transfusions were ordered. I was in such anguish that I can't recall all that was done in their efforts to try to keep Brian alive. All I could do was pray.

He was given eight pints of blood before they finally got the crisis under control. We came close to losing him that terrible day, but we didn't—even to the doctors' surprise.

Our family prayed, our church prayed, his young friends at the Christian academy where Brian had been attending prayed, and many others who learned of his condition prayed. We were informed that there were prayers from churches and temples and synagogues that went up for him from many directions.

Individuals who heard of his situation, one way or the other, would come to visit him or send him a card to let him know how much they cared. They assured him that they were praying for him. There was never a day someone wasn't by his side to encourage and speak words of faith and comfort to Brian, and there was never a day when prayers didn't ascend heavenward on his behalf.

I would go to intensive care—and then to his room when he was finally moved—and find religious symbols and medals of all sorts pinned to his pillow or on his bed or his table. I was so grateful for them all. Anything that anyone sent that had their love and care associated with it I considered a material form of prayer and saw that it was kept near my child.

I truly believe that love and trust are the most powerful forces in the universe. They are powerful enough that, despite the terrible prognosis, three months later, we eventually brought Brian home—off the ventilator and in a wheelchair.

One of the doctors told me later that, "off the record," what he observed happen with Brian was a "damn miracle." He said he had seen kids not as seriously injured as Brian who never made it off the respirator—let alone make it home.

I, for one, believe in prayer and in miracles. How could I not?

I smile sometimes looking at Brian and knowing that forty years later, some of those very doctors whose pronouncements back then sent us to our knees have themselves died. Brian is now sixty years old, and he has remained a witness to the sustaining power of faith and an example of courage.

Brian's quiet wisdom, great faith, and generous heart have helped so many people throughout his years, and they continue to do so, especially his mother. He inspires me every day to believe in something greater than what I can see or experience.

My spirit sighs and I say, "Amazing Grace."

Today, although my son can no longer embrace me, I have him near. I can still hug him and kiss his cheek, which I often do. We can still laugh and talk, travel, play games, dine together, and spend happy, grateful days together.

As one of those old plaques that hung on my mother's walls stated: "Prayer changes things." Today, whenever I look at Brian, I think of all the miracles that had to take place in order for heaven to keep him by my side—and I have to admit that it surely does.

Leona with son. Brian

# 29
# The Women in My Life

So many of the women who have made up my experiences in this world are gone now. All were sweet fragrances that linger, but some were as glorious as blossoming sunflowers in the garden of my life.

I recall their many lovely faces smiling back at me—my mother, sisters, aunts, cousins, daughters, and friends. They come to me in pleasant dreams or my quiet reflective moments and grace my existence still.

Alfred Lord Tennyson said, "It's better to have loved and lost than never to have loved at all." There is no greater truth, my reasoning soul admits. I'm so glad I knew their loveliness no matter the brief calculation of their days my broken heart has determined. Only forever with them would have been enough.

I miss the era my women and I have known together. I miss the understanding. I miss the nods of agreement. I miss the looks in their eyes that come from sharing the same or similar experiences.

Yes! I dearly miss those who taught me so much of life through their own victories and pain and their noble ability to rise above it all. They were—both young and old—my heroes and inspiration. I long to hear again those familiar voices who spoke to me in common tones of things we knew together. Those who comforted me with the touch of both their hand and voice.

The river of time has widened greatly between those distant shores of days that we once walked together. But, now, so many of my lovely women are *over there*—and I am still *over here*. And the once clear sounds of their voices now grow dimmer in my listening ears.

So many times, I guess you know, I wish I could pick up the phone and dial their number once again so I could hear them on the other end. There are questions I need their help to answer and memories I need them to help me recall.

That's the problem with being a survivor and enjoying a richness of years: everything has a price we have to pay.

The listening hearts that were once the sounding boards for me can no longer respond. The voices that were once my source of reason and comfort—or the ones who were always the generous providers of either wisdom or laughter—are no longer present. I have become increasingly aware of a growing silence in portions of my life.

A few months down the road, I'll be eighty years old. At this blessed age, there are few, understandably, who remain to wander down memory lane with me. And so, I have lost a large portion of myself because of my beautiful women's absences.

But that's the way it is. It's what happens when so many goodbyes accumulate for us. However, we cannot stay in our mourning clothes for too long because the heavenly timekeeper's bell will soon sound, and it will be our own mortal door closing onto this world. Then we will have become someone else's "lost woman."

Sometimes, I want to tell the young women in my own life to ask me things while I can still give them an answer. Despite our strongest bonds, life—and everything in it—changes.

Ask me now, my loves, while I can still hear your sweet voices—and while you can still hear mine. Soon, I, too, will finally have sailed away and joined my other women across the ocean of time.

# 30
# A True Legacy

You can leave your children a lot of things, but certain things are priceless.

I'm remembering a dear friend of mine who lost her battle to cancer right after I moved from New Jersey to Florida. The lessons of her last days have remained with me.

In November 2009, just weeks before she died, my friend stopped to visit me at my house in New Jersey. I was delighted and surprised to see her. She was very fragile by that time. The cancer had won, but she was still fighting valiantly to be purposeful.

Seeing that I was home, she waved off her daughter who had brought her there. "Just thought I would see how you were coming along with your packing for your move to Florida—and see if you had time for some tea and a sandwich and a chat." That was something she and I had done so many times for over forty years.

Tragically, her waning days were coinciding with my need to leave the state to be near our disabled son, Brian, who had recently undergone life-threatening surgery.

He had survived, but he was forty-nine, and we knew we needed to be living near him and not just traveling there several times a year.

I knew the visit I would have with my old friend that day might be the last time I saw her on earth. I hugged her and welcomed her in warmly. "I'll put on the pot," I responded with a smile.

My friend owned little of value in this world. She had been born into poverty and never rose very far in life from where she had begun.

After a short while, I could see there was something troubling her mind, and so, as friends often do, I probed her thinking. On that last day we spent together, I discovered that she was wrestling with some regrets. She was sad, she confessed, that she had nothing to leave to her children.

I thought of how self-reliant, honest, sympathetic, and generous her children were—just like her. Widowed very young, she had raised them on her own. A couple of them were now successful, and the others had learned by example from her how to cope with the ups and downs of life's fortunes and failures.

In those last few months of her life, I had never seen such sweetness, kindness, courage, and faith. She had suffered so much, but she tried her best to not overwhelm those who were caring for her. Her heart ached with a loving mother's sympathy for her children's fear of losing her.

I was amazed by how easy it was for me to determine her children's inheritance. Yet, in her hours of dwindling opportunities to repair anything done or left undone, she only saw her lack of anything of material value to distribute to them.

I sent up a silent prayer that I could find the right words to bring my dear dying friend some peace. "Please make this last conversation count, Lord," I pleaded.

In that troubled moment, I wanted her to see that she had given her five children gifts of immeasurable value.

As my thoughts mined the years and their scenes, I knew her whole life had been a gift to the many who had known her beautiful nature. The lessons she had given to many of us through the great courage she had demonstrated in her patient coping with suffering were beyond measure.

Her life had revealed a nature full of self-sacrificing kindness and a faith that didn't fail her. Her deeply held beliefs had amazingly lifted her above fear and self-pity. Through it all, her children and grandchildren had been shown the unbroken beauty of a mother and grandmother's devotion.

Nothing to bequeath to them? Ha! I knew in my heart that her family, from having had her in their lives, was richer than kings! Everyone should be given such treasures.

"Your children were blessed the moment life placed them in your arms," I said. "They're all decent adults who know how to survive, how to be good parents, and how to deal with tough times, and they help and care for one another as you always urged them to do, don't they?"

She smiled when I said that. "Yes, that's true, isn't it?"

We went down memory lane for a while. I was moved when she told me, with tears, that she knew God had been looking out for her when he brought me into her life. She didn't want to think how tough it might have been without me! I assured her that God knew we would both need each other—for many reasons.

I looked at her and realized, once more, how much I had loved and needed this brave, unselfish little woman in my life. She was a simple, humble, and uncomplicated person who forever thought I had answers enough for both of us. All along, she had been much wiser than she knew.

"Listen," I finally said, "you may not realize it, but you have given your children a priceless gift—a gift that not many get to receive. This is a world filled with so many things to battle and fear—and nothing quite as fearful as our own deaths. Many parents can teach their children how to live bravely, but you, my love, have shown your children how to *die* bravely. More than that, you have shared that rare power of the human spirit that you own with many more people than I think you're aware of, including me. Honey, your life has been a treasure to all who've been fortunate enough to know you. Your very self has been the legacy you leave behind."

I looked at her and remembered how she had loved to bring me gifts. No occasion was ever necessary. She just loved giving and making others happy. Her gifts to me over the years are still among my favorite things.

So, it wasn't strange, I realize, that she would be concerned that day about whether she had given enough before she left this world. I know I inherited wonderful memories of the years we shared. She left us all richer by her existence.

And so, my dear friend, wherever you are in timeless moments, in some place that I know is brightened by your presence, I want you to know that your gifts have all been lasting ones. Your spirit was the precious legacy we can still enjoy whenever we speak your name.

# 31
# *Chaos and Order*

I recall reading a fascinating book by a physicist who spoke about the two dynamic forces at work throughout the universe: chaos and order. He mentioned that every atom that exists is being manipulated by either one or the other.

It was informative to realize everything we do contributes to the aim of one of these two. For instance, when we participate in doing constructive, productive things, we direct positive energy toward correcting, preventing, or holding back the negative energy of chaos.

With that thought in mind, we need to be vigilant in our efforts to be a part of those things orderly because chaos is always trying to return things to a disorderly state of existence.

Ever cleared an area of briars? I grew up in the country, so I know that even after cutting them down to the ground, if you don't stay on top of controlling them, you'll quickly have those tough vines with sharp stickers growing over everything else in the area. Some things are aggressively unpleasant and persistent. We must match ourselves to them.

Lily Tomlin said she had heard of a serious need somewhere and thought, *Boy, somebody ought to do something about that! Wait a minute! I am that somebody!* That's the level of understanding we must reach to begin applying our contribution to order.

We each, as individuals, have a role, however small it may be, in making our home, community, or the world a better, more stable, environmentally improved, and safer place to live in today and with concern for the future.

Peace is a product of order. We need to work together as best we can with the rest of humankind to try to hold things together for one another. We learned in grammar school that every action has a reaction. With the awareness that, at any given time, we are an element in all things concerning either chaos or order, we don't have to be physicists to know which force we tend to support with our actions.

# 32
# Self-Encouragement

We have experiences that disturb our best intentions for ourselves; these disruptive forces pound upon our souls like gale winds and blow our spirits off course. Our reactions often can be primal. We have great directive energy within, and it sometimes gets released in a chaotic rather than a reasonable manner.

Chaos and order are always at war in all of nature—and in us. All we can do is stay true to our dominant intents, gather ourselves together again, accept the ancient human who lives within us, and seek to quiet their fears and find comfort for their tears. It's not an easy task managing this experience of being a conscious, sensory being in a universe we don't understand with only the armor of our reason, wits, and perceptions to protect and lead us. So be patient and forgiving of yourself on those occasions when you "let the dogs out." It's your life and your dogs. You'll get them back in again.

Then, once a semblance of order kicks in, let go of the acts or words of the primal you—just as you would for a friend.

Our singular existence throughout, from sandbox to pine box, is a self-editing thing. Even at my advanced age, I'm still giving myself pep talks on handling things in some ideal way that I've noted should be the right way to go. I don't anticipate ever getting to that nearly perfect place in life.

Thank goodness I believe in heaven's grace, which I hold to compensate for my frequent failings.

I try to see each new day as a *resurrection* of our weary spirits, a new opportunity for finding our hoped-for charted course, a new gift of awareness in which we sense we have become freshly clothed with greater light, and a new infusion of determination to find the path back to our better choices.

People say, "Tough times don't last, but tough people do." I agree, but that can only be the case if we struggling human beings keep pushing ourselves toward another better day, moving away from the weaknesses and troubles of yesterday with all the courage and opportunity that life allows us. We must look within ourselves for the strength and determination to meet the challenges of just one day and one experience at a time. Dogs—and disasters—be damned!

# 33
## Psalm 138:3

In the day when I cried, you answered me and strengthened me.

Our children Merry, Robert, Dane and Brian in 1964

# 34
# Events Related to My Children

I married young. I gave birth to seven children. I lost four of those children between 1963 and 2018.

In 1963, Leona Bernice died at five years old from problems related to a brain injury that occurred during delivery.

In 1982, Dane Preston died at twenty-one in an auto accident.

In 1992, Kelly Kathleen died at twenty-five from liver disease.

In 2018, Robert William died at fifty-eight from a lifetime of alcohol and drug abuse.

I've chosen not to include the details of each of these experiences in this volume, but because so many years of our lives were dedicated to our youngest child's illness and our struggles with it, I've written about it in the next part.

# 35
## Losing Kelly

I was always losing Kelly.

I still can clearly remember that terrible day when Kelly was still a toddler. I took her shopping at a huge flea market near our home. It was only open on Tuesdays. It was comprised of several buildings, and inside each one, there were merchant's stalls lining each side of the walls, plus additional ones down the center of the buildings. They represented lots of bargains for a young mother on a budget to consider. It was very popular and attracted thousands of people.

On that particular day, I stopped at a table that caught my eye and reached to pick up an item. I briefly let go of Kelly's hand. With my peripheral vision, I noted a small child I thought was Kelly moving around beside me, so I continued checking merchandise. When I finally reached to take the hand of the child beside me, she pulled away and spun toward her own mother. I gasped and realized my horrendous mistake! Oh, dear God, *it wasn't my Kelly!* And Kelly was nowhere to be seen in the crowd!

I immediately went into a panic. I wept as I pushed feverishly through the crowd, calling her name at the top of my lungs. "Kelly! Kelly! Where are you, honey?" My mind screamed. *Please, God, don't let anything happen to Kelly. Please let me find her. Please!*

Moaning as I spoke rapidly to merchants and strangers alike, I repeated my question over and over: "Have you seen a little light-haired, blue-eyed four-year-old?" I then raced away when they shook their heads.

I ran through the building and called her name, crazed with the fear that some unkind stranger might have lured my beautiful trusting baby away from me forever.

I was almost at the point of physical and emotional collapse when I heard her voice call out, "There's my mommy. Right there!" Kelly was pointing me out to the worried lady who was holding her hand.

I don't know how many times I said thank you to that wonderful woman who thought the best thing to do was to just stay where they were, hold on to Kelly, and wait until some insane woman like me came along. So, with my fear melting into tears of relief, I knelt and pulled my small child into my arms, not wanting to ever let go of her for fear that I might lose her again.

"Mommy," Kelly said, wiping at my tears, "I was looking for you."

"Yes, honey, I know," I told her. "We were looking for each other. We're okay now. But you must promise Mommy you'll never leave me like that ever again. I was so scared."

"Okay, Mommy," she said, and she hugged my neck again.

It was a promise Kelly would not be able to keep for long.

Quick and alert, Kelly didn't miss a thing that went on around her. While still a toddler, I once located her atop the washer in the laundry room. She had taken note of where I had stashed a package of cookies in the overhead cabinets. In her quest to get at them, she had located my step stool in the closet, dragged it over in front of the washer, opened it, and managed to use it to climb onto the top of the washer.

When I found her, she was standing precariously and loading her pockets with her find.

I moved quickly toward her and scooped her up, grateful she hadn't injured herself in her determination to get to the cookies. I told her she shouldn't have climbed up there the way she did because she might have gotten hurt. "You should have come and gotten Mommy to help you with the cookies," I said.

"No! I can do it myself, Mommy," she asserted.

There was much she would teach me that she could handle on her own.

Yet, inside me, there remained this inexplicable nagging concern about my ability to keep this child of mine safe. Call it mother's intuition if you will.

In January 1973, after the United States signed the Paris Peace Accord ending the war in Vietnam, the world seemed a little more stable. Kelly was seven years old. We packed all our children into the station wagon to take them to Disney World in Florida. It was a great idea.

The trip proved to be even more fun than we anticipated—one of the best times of our lives—but Kelly kept us all on our toes as we tried keeping up with her delight at everything she saw. She raced ahead of us, it seemed, from morning until night, charging us with the constant plea, "Come on, hurry up, everybody. Come on, come on, please."

"Kelly, get back here! You're going to get lost," I repeated more often than I can remember. I hated to dampen their vacation enthusiasm, but I implored her siblings not to let their baby sister out of their sight. I had never forgotten the painful episode of losing her at the flea market when she was four.

Three years later, we headed back to the Magic Kingdom. The second trip was no exception as far as Kelly's wanderlust was concerned. It was still a challenge to not let Kelly slip away from us. She appeared to have some inner urgency to see everything as fast as she could.

On our last day, as Kelly stood holding the rail on one of the little boats that ferried the guests back and forth from the parking area to the Magic Kingdom, our oldest daughter, Merry, said, "Mom, have you noticed how funny Kelly's skin looks?" I hadn't. I took Kelly's face in my hands and studied it in the Florida sun. Her skin and her eyes were a greenish-yellow. She was jaundiced.

The best name they could give to her condition was *acute chronic incurable liver disease*—of unknown origin. Her blood wouldn't clot well enough to perform surgery. The doctors' frightening prognosis was that she would not live another year. I refused to accept that I was going to lose my daughter. We were going to fight to keep her here! We drew out our savings and took Kelly anywhere we thought there might be a promise of hope. We spent countless hours—days, weeks, and months—researching and trying to uncover some new regimen or wonder diet that might keep us from losing Kelly. Some of it must have worked because she didn't die within that year. Or the next few. I don't know how Kelly found the courage to endure all she did or how someone so young lived with the frightening knowledge that her body was letting her down.

Instead of self-pity, Kelly was kind and giving. She was always full of smiles and gratitude for the sacrifices her family was making for her. She lived so fearlessly and positively that it quelled some of our own anxiety. Because of her attitude, there would be days we let our weary minds think maybe we wouldn't lose her after all.

In her late teens, although she had lived several years beyond the doctors' earlier conclusions, Kelly seemed to develop a sense of dwindling time. She didn't say it, but it was expressed in the things she began to do.

With all the maternal empathy I could muster, I still could not relate to what Kelly was going through or the mental strategies she needed to wrestle against this thief of a young girl's life and dreams. I only knew that I kept losing her.

It would happen like this. Moments before she'd disappear, she might be sitting on the porch petting her cat, Vanna. I would turn to ask her something, and she would be gone. Just like that. Without a word or an explanation. She would just walk off and be gone. When we saw her again—hours or even days later—I would ask her why she did such things.

"I just needed to go, Mom," she would say. "If I tried to explain it to you, you would get upset."

She was right. I would have tried to keep her from going. So it was easier for her to say nothing and just leave.

"But where were you?" I might ask. "I called all around, and no one had seen you. I know you're grown, but I'm still your mom—and I worry. How would I know if something happened to you?"

"Oh, Mom!" she would reply softly. "I think we can agree that something has happened to me, but I was fine. I just wandered over to Aunt Martha and Uncle Donald's place and rode Lisa's horse, Sam, around in the field. They weren't home, but they've told me plenty of times to just come over whenever I like and exercise Sam. Lisa has a new horse blanket, so I slept in the barn last night and ate some apples off their tree. You always tell me that my angels are watching over me, don't you?" With that, she would turn and head toward her bedroom. "I'm going to take a shower and maybe watch *Wheel of Fortune*. Okay?"

Sometimes, when I must have looked extremely troubled by the events, she would come back, throw her arms around my neck, and tell me that I was the best mom in the whole world. She would tell me she was sorry she had caused so much trouble for me, but she needed the freedom to break free and go whenever she felt the need to go.

More than once, she would emotionally say, "Please try to understand, Mom. Please!"

"Okay," I would reluctantly say—but only because it was what she needed me to do. I didn't understand.

As Kelly aged into her twenties, during the times when she would be at home, I was very cautious about her diet to avoid taxing her liver. I did everything I could to aid her failing immune system. I made her fresh fruit and vegetable juices and homemade whole grain breads, and I kept the pantry filled with wholesome food. There were times when she was better than others, and those occasions of relief kept me trying.

She found comfort in my many attentions, but the urge to leave would return—and I would prayerfully await her return.

When Kelly wasn't wandering, the times we spent together were happy ones. We cooked, painted, sewed, planted, enjoyed time with her sibling's children, and spent pleasant moments having long talks over cups of tea.

I was always offering hope of some new approach to her illness, and she would sweetly pretend to believe me. One of her favorite comforts was lying across my lap on the sofa and asking me questions about my life as I scratched her back. Perhaps she lived vicariously through my "normal" life as a woman with a home and a family, which she knew she would probably never get to experience—or perhaps it was just part of her clinging to her mother. There was never any doubt of how much she loved me.

Then, in September 1992, she developed what seemed to be a bad cold. She was very weak and had problems walking. As I was rubbing some Vicks on her chest as she lay on the sofa, she leaned up and kissed my cheek. "I'm not afraid of dying, Mom," she said softly. "I'll just miss you doing things like this for me."

Fighting tears, I scolded her gently for even considering that it would happen any time soon.

She didn't press the point. She just smiled that sweet smile of hers.

Distressed by her comment, I slept on the other sofa to be near her that night, and I called the doctor first thing in the morning. He thought it might be better if she was treated in the hospital. I realize now that she knew she wasn't leaving that hospital, but she kept up a bright, cheerful appearance for the family as we gathered around her bed daily.

Kelly gave me her rings to take home one day while I was visiting.

"Will you take care of them for me till I come home?" she asked. "Just so nothing happens to them in here."

With a great surge of fear, I slid her rings off her hands and onto my own fingers.

"Don't get too used to them," she said with a smile, encouraging my belief that she would be wearing them at home again soon.

I nodded. "I'll have them cleaned up for you," I said as I kissed her cheek. I wasn't prepared for the possibility that my world might not have Kelly in it.

Then, one day when I was running late for my hospital visit with her, she called me on the phone. "Why aren't you here, Mom? Don't you miss me?" she asked.

"Not miss you?" I replied with a chuckle. "Kelly, I've been missing you your whole life."

Even with that sad truth stated, we both laughed.

On September 28, 1992, we were awakened during the night with a call from the hospital to go there immediately. Kelly's situation had turned critical.

She was on a respirator by the time we got there.

I stood by her hospital bed and brushed her forehead while softly imploring her once again not to leave me. But I knew she had to go.

I wept unconsolably as I held onto her hand. Because, this time, I had just lost my Kelly for the last time.

Kelly with her brother, Jesse and niece, Lara

# 36
## Grief

The very process of grief, when you have survived it, brings you out on the other side altered by it—whether others recognize it or not. And your specific relationship to the one you lost determines the shaping qualities of grief's carvings on your soul and your nature.

# 37
## Mother Said

My mother said that other people can't make you happy because happiness is a by-product of your own philosophy and perspective on life. Situations and experiences can provide pleasure, which is short-lived, but the real thing comes from assessing your life and gaining an appreciation and acceptance of who you are. It is associated with a deep sense of gratitude for all you have received of life's bounty and a persuasion that you have a connectedness to the eternal. When you have reached that point in your understanding—where you have a knowledge of the difference between those things of real enduring value and all the rest of it—you will have discovered the true mother of happiness: joy.

# 38
## Your Journey

I've learned that being on a path that seeks awareness, light, and hope doesn't mean you'll be spared traveling those paths of darkness, pain, regret, and self-discouragement. In truth, your journey may be one that drives you to your knees many times. However, in those places of pain and darkness—when you are bowed and broken by trouble and tears—your spirit may open to a new awareness, and it becomes a place of wisdom for you. That has so often been the case for me.

Only the One who has mapped out your development like the path of the humble acorn to becoming the mighty oak tree controls the applying of the forces that will make you become what you were meant to become.

You are not your own—even though you may sometimes feel that way. There is an ideal result for which you were conceived: a magnificent you that is beyond what you can imagine today. Only the One who holds the plans is aware of the final product. Allow that trust to bring you patience and peace.

As with every part and parcel of the universe, you are always in a state of *becoming*.

We are the clay, not the Potter.

No matter where you are on your path through life, my friend, hold onto the trust that the same Power that holds the stars and planets in place is capable of holding you as well.

I am of a stronger mind and spirit in my old age than I was in my youth. I have been lifted and guided and restored to strength and purpose time and time again.

Your life experience—your timeless spirit—is to be an endless journey of lessons and awareness and new wisdom and connections. Each step you take will involve discovering more of what life really is. As you make your own unique way along the road of time, you'll discover that the Eternal Presence will lead and inform you and become the source of all your strength and peace.

We only lose our way on our journey when we lose faith in our Guide.

# 39
# A Perfect Match

Life has shown me that a close, beautiful friendship doesn't have to be about "equals." It doesn't have to be about similar backgrounds, intellect, or means. It doesn't have to have any relationship to politics, religion, or race. Friendship just is.

Sometimes friendship just springs up as though you had always known that person, and sometimes it just grows slowly to become what it is.

As I look back over my life, I realize that many dear friendships that spanned decades seemed at first to have happened simply by chance. However, the years and the many experiences we shared proved these people surely were meant to be part of the fabric of my life.

I remember having a brief conversation with a woman who was so unaware of her own offensiveness that she asked me what I could possibly have in common with a precious gal who had become almost like a sister to me.

*Really?* I couldn't believe she could ask such an unseemly question. I have to admit that in that moment, I wanted to smack her hard. Instead, I looked at her and knew she didn't have a clue as to what friendship was all about. I stemmed my impulses and said, "Not a thing—except for the deep love we have for one another." And then I walked away.

It was true that my friend and I were different in so many ways, but how I loved her beautiful heart! Her efforts on everyone's behalf were endless. She forgave every unkindness.

My friend was always a devil's advocate, a sympathetic listening ear, and a go-to open door for every troubled life. Although she had so little herself, she was generous to a fault. She could make others smile even when she had so much to cry about.

Her faith was pure, simple, and boundless.

My foolish, shallow questioner didn't know any of these things about my friend. She only knew whisperings about my friend's disadvantaged station in life, her level of education, or how she dressed in used clothing and lived in subsidized housing. I knew the woman questioning me that day was a church member, so I could have drawn parallels to Jesus's life concerning similar descriptions, but I didn't. Anyway, on that basic information regarding my friend, the question was shaped. She couldn't possibly see how my friend and I would be as comfortable as we were in each other's company. And for so many years!

Ha! I kind of felt sorry for that woman, but at the same time, I was grateful for my own rich life. Such an unfortunate, silly person. I could see she had missed many opportunities for warm and loving experiences in life. In her ignorance and puzzled considerations, I realized that what some people like her called "friendship" would never pass muster with me.

The Good Book says, "In order to have friends, a man must show himself to be friendly." Amen.

Shortly before she left this world my friend told me one more time that she was so glad that she had lived most of her life with me in it as her friend and that she hoped somehow in God's great plan that we'd meet again in another place and time.

I responded by letting her know that I had not a single doubt that heaven had made magnets of our hearts and souls that would bring us together again—someplace where destiny would continue to guide us.

"Love never ends," I said tearfully, reminding her of the promise scripture makes to us. "And I love you, little sister."

When holidays come around, I can't help but reflect on all the special gifts I've known in the forms of beautiful people. There have been so very many.

Heaven must really like me because some of its very best human creations have been given to me as life enhancing friendships. In my grateful heart, it seems there have been way too many to be just coincidences. When I pray, I express how very grateful I am.

Listen when I advise you to always keep your heart alert. You just never know where the love of beautiful friendship might be waiting for you. Perhaps like most of mine have been, the two of you may be a perfect match.

# 40
# The Gift of Jesse

I have always felt that the Great Someone watches over my husband, Jesse, perhaps partly in answer to my prayers. Perhaps it's because he's also Irish, like me, and thereby lucky. He certainly has had some unusual and dramatic close calls. Who knows? I only know that, despite the several times we feared we would lose him, he is still here where I can look across the room at him as he lives on happily and handsomely.

All four of his brothers were lost to genetic cardiovascular problems—one at only forty-two years old—but Jesse is still with me after almost fifty-six years of marriage. That's sure beating some tough odds.

Also, three of his four sisters have passed.

I often ask myself how I could have carried life's burdens of losing four children—plus the added pain of these forty-two years since Brian's accident, which left him severely disabled—and do it all without Jesse? I don't even want to contemplate that scenario!

I know without a doubt, there are people who have been gifts to our lives! How fortunate for us that they were.

In this thing we call life, we all have our own unique mixed bags of blessings and losses. We must never lose sight of the former while we're coping with the latter. Jesse has been one of my great blessings.

And so, despite all the tragic events and tears I have known throughout the years, I thank heaven that, through it all, I've had this wonderful helpmate by my side.

We need to always be mindful of the shaping work of both blessings and losses on our human lives. To do so helps us remain dynamic, stable, and strong. I'm glad I've been spared the pain and struggle of loneliness as I've faced the tragic circumstances of my days—thanks to my gift of Jesse!

Leona with husband, Jesse

# 41
# The Mystery of Enduring Love

> All things may pass away but these three remain: faith,
> hope and love. But the greatest of these is love.
> —1 Corinthians 13:13

I am always awed when my heart and mind—in humblest gratitude—studies the miracle of love. I have discovered over my lifetime—even when we're devoid of hope, even when our faith has faltered, and even when our will to raise our heads up off our pillow has fled us—that there will still exist around us those who would pour upon us endless tributes of their unfailing devotion. They are holding onto us because of the unrelenting power of their love.

This magnificent mystery we call love, which surely was made manifest to us in creative design for the care and nurture of our human bodies and spirits while we yet exist, is a part of the fabric of the universe and the web that keeps all things connected.

I must tell you that it is a humbling concept for me to ponder when I, in wonder, consider how far-reaching its streams flow over unbounded time. I am certain there will be those who, despite all our human frailties, will never stop loving us—even when death has taken us from their sight and eternal reach.

In my emotional inventory of memories, I think of the enduring love that is still within my heart for my mother, father, brothers, sisters, friends, and four precious children who have each passed beyond love's physical touch. The heart cannot untwine that Gordian knot that was knit between my heart and theirs alone. They exist as though they are within the very cells of my life force. It seems to the depth of my soul that they'll be with me to the end of this stage of living and then will be there to escort me onward with them on the rest of the journey.

This reality of love endows us with reasons for loving that should be unreasonable. Reason, it seems, would cap love's flow at the graveside since there is no longer a recipient of its force. And yet, its power will not be abated.

And so, we testify that what the scriptures say is true: "The greatest of these is love." All we can say about this great eternal mystery is this: "How divine!"

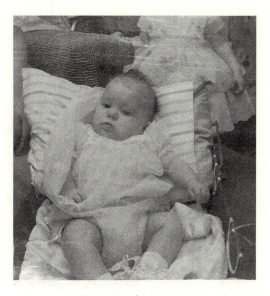

Our Little Leona

# 42
## Keeping Dreams Alive

Please, don't be a destroyer of dreams—
not your own or anyone else's.
Dreams are too hard to come by,
And harder yet to make come true.
It seems extremely sad to me
For something to die inside a person
While they're still alive.

Leona Flowers

# 43
# Taking My Father to Ireland

When Bing Crosby sang the theme song from the movie, *The Bells of Saint Mary's*, in 1945, it immediately became one of my Irish Catholic father's favorite songs, especially since the old stone church of Saint Mary's in the town of Salem, New Jersey, was his own chosen house of prayer for many years before his death.

He added the song to his repertoire, and with his strong, marvelous voice, he would sing it to me as he lulled me to sleep or entertained me with it as I rode beside him in our horse and wagon headed somewhere along a country road.

I loved those moments with my father.

He also knew and sang what seemed like every popular Irish tune and taught them to me as well. As my thoughts go to him, as they so often do, I still sing or hum them today. He always sang as he worked; it was as though the words in those songs lifted and carried his heart and mind to other pleasant places and times. He never spoke much about religious things, but I know my father's faith went deep because of how he lived. I remember him laughing, smiling, singing, and never complaining—not even as the cancer ravaged him during his last days. His spirit was so strong that in 1950, when I was a ten-year old child, I recognized he was sick, weak, and unable to do the work he had always done, but I was never truly aware of how really sick he was or that he was dying. And no one thought it would be good to tell me.

I never knew how long he had owned his rosary beads or where he had obtained them. I only know they were probably his most cherished possession. My mother had told me they weren't jewelry and that I shouldn't play with them. She explained how Daddy took them to church with him and held them when he prayed.

And so, sensing the special role those beads with a crucifix on them played in my father's religious life, I never did anything other than look at them. Each night, he hung his rosary carefully over a crucifix about eight inches high, made entirely from wooden matchsticks. Each morning, they went into his pocket as he dressed and prepared himself to face the cares or joys of the day.

As often as he was able to, he would go to early-morning Mass before he started his day's work. I know now that he found the hope and courage he needed to handle his painful life while down there on his knees, rosary in hand, within the sacred walls of Saint Mary's.

How do I adequately express from the heart of the child I was so long ago, now replaced by this aged woman, how I realize it was surely the love and joy my father brought into my earliest days that helped shield my view of the harsher realities that pervaded our existence? How could I possibly compare that smiling superman of my youth with anyone else?

Despite the reality and the hardships he encountered, I recognize that in my psyche, he stood like a rock between me and the specter of fear because my father's happy, hopeful nature full of stories and songs kept me mostly happy as well.

My father and I also shared a sweet secret: something special in his thoughts. I knew of a dream he held. I don't know if even my mother was aware because, had she known, she might have thought it was a foolish thing for him to consider, and worse, to share such an impossibility with me.

I loved hearing him speak hopefully of the possibility of this dream coming true. He encouraged me to think that life *does* have magic in it— and that we should speak of wonderful possibilities. He established within me a belief that our hopes and dreams have the power to lift us far above the often-dreary realness of our days and fill our imaginations with smiles. His perfect dream was to travel to Ireland someday.

His father, Anthony Dean, had immigrated to America as a young man with his parents from Galway, Ireland, in the late 1800s. My father's grandparents and father loved their homeland and evidently often reminisced of it to my father as he was growing up. Their description of this enchanted land across the sea was enough to have planted in him an ardent desire to see Ireland for himself. It was a desire that never dissipated no matter how old or ill he became. Instead, it only grew stronger as the years and his youth passed.

I loved my father to the extent that when he spoke of traveling to Ireland someday, I felt his dream as well, and I wished it for him with all the longings my young heart could muster. I wanted my dear father to be as happy as he made me.

But it was never to be. He and his dream ended on July 17, 1950. His eyes were never to see Ireland's beautiful shores except in those moments when it existed in his life's lovely imaginings.

Yet, when I was seventy-five years old, a remarkable event occurred. My grandson, Miles Teller, helped me take my father there. In a way.

Miles had grown up hearing the stories of his great-grandfather, my father, James Joseph Dean. He knew that I, too, had hoped someday, like my father, to see Ireland and the city of Galway in particular.

In 2015, as an anniversary gift, from his magnificent awareness of what would make his grandmother extremely happy, Miles announced to me that he would be taking his grandfather and me on a planned trip around Ireland! He was planning on traveling with us to the land of his great-grandfather's dream.

I was thrilled beyond measure. I was so happy at the thought of it that the old woman I had become wept, and the little girl who still lived within me jumped for joy.

My father hadn't been able to take me there with him, but sixty-five years later, my grandson would be doing it for him—and for me.

As I prepared for the upcoming journey, a plan that made me smile came to mind. I went into my photo albums and looked for a certain picture. I finally found it.

The picture was taken in 1948. It is a blurry photo of my father and me. We're in front of that old house we lived in. It's an image of stark poverty. He is shirtless and barefoot. I am small and clinging to him. His arm is around me, holding me near.

Later, before we packed to leave for Ireland, I enlarged and printed out the picture, rolled it into a scroll, put it in a sealed container with a green ribbon wrapped around it, and stashed it in my luggage.

In Galway, Ireland, we thrilled at knowing that for generations our forebears had walked these streets, operated businesses, and played an important role in the ebb and flow of their times and communities. My father had told me that the Deans had been an important family there. We discovered that in the center of the town where the names and crests of the Twelve Tribes of Galway stood, sure enough, there was one with our Dean family name on it.

How I wished that my father could have laid his eyes on that.

As we explored its lovely streets, we also happily discovered a centuries-old, beautiful Catholic church. It was named Saint Mary's.

How could I not feel we had been led there?

On the day before we left Galway, we watched as my husband, Jesse, dug a spot in a small flower garden that grew against the back of that ancient stone church. I wept as I planted the picture I had carried there. At least an image of him could now rest in the land of his dreams. And so, with tears and smiles, we said goodbye to my dear father at his beloved St. Mary's.

I can't express the sense of joy and fulfillment that went through my soul at that moment. I could almost hear Bing Crosby singing that wonderful song about St. Mary's bells and imagine that angels were smiling. It was just that profound for me.

As I walked away, I felt all the sweetness of the happy days I had known at my father's side as he sang and showed his little girl the power of someone's dreams—and the divine power of St. Mary's on his soul.

In that remarkable moment there in Ireland, I felt that through that part of him that still lived on in us, my grandson and I, through our own personal pilgrimage and experience, had brought my father to this place of his heart's longings.

And I just felt that somewhere, where other fields were green, my father was surely smiling.

Leona and grandson, Miles Teller, enjoying being Irish

# 44
## Bullying

When I was a child, my father gave me lessons in standing up to bullies. I guess he thought his little girl might need them. Maybe he thought because I was starting out with so little in life that the world would believe I was at its mercy. In any case, he and my proud mother built such a backbone in me that I always stood up for myself as I grew—and I also defended anyone else who came to me for aid.

Later in life, as a young wife and mother, I came to earn the title in my small town of "the poor woman's lawyer." That was because, with pen and clipboard in hand, I would accompany women who needed my ability to communicate well, to welfare offices, family services offices, and even before judges to make appeals on their behalf. I hated to see anyone made afraid of individuals or systems that might seek to abuse power.

My dad taught me to push back against bullies of all sorts.

Now, I want to love folks and be able to trust people to do the right thing, to be fair and kind and not take advantage of whatever rank they may hold over someone else, but I know that isn't always possible.

I learned basic human psychology from that salesman father of mine. He had come to a lot of conclusions about why people do what they do based on all the people he had had exchanges with over his life.

My father said I would meet some people who would be so nice that I would want to help them in whatever way I could and give them all the breaks, but I would also meet others who would be so mean, that other "breaks" would spring to my mind where they were concerned. All of which I soon found to be true.

Life cast me as the youngest into a large family with lots of opportunities for human interaction right from the start. There were lots of lessons in interpersonal relationships in that big mix, but my dad also tried to instill skills in me for engaging with the larger world.

My dad spoke to me of experiences that involved some bullying he had endured in his own boyhood in Philly. He wanted me to be aware that not everyone would allow me to be pleasant or even welcome it.

He told me to be aware of bullying's subtler forms as well. Someone might not put their hands on you, but they will still be pushing you in one way or another or seeking to control your responses or actions. He instilled an acute awareness in me that's still in there.

To this day, when I recognize bullying being applied, the Irish in me boils up, and I become as resistant and stubborn as that biblical mule of Balaam's.

However, a soft tone and a loving, gentle approach are my Achilles' heel. You'll land me with your sweetness. I will usually wear myself to the bone when kindness and reasonable appeal are the carrots one is using.

So, I've found that those bits of advice my father shared with me in my childhood regarding bullies to be true: with some folks, an attitude of pleasantness is foreign to their nature. So be it.

If anyone foolishly considers bullying as a tactic to urge me in some direction other than that of my own choosing, well, they may be talking, but they'll soon discover they're only talking to my back.

# 45
# *Friendship*

I was thinking this morning of the amazing friendships I have known throughout my years. These special people entered my life and carried me through so many tough places or just brought laughter when I needed it.

There are things I have learned about friendship from each of their lovely presences in my world. A friend is someone who draws out the best in you. Friends help make you aware of your potential so that you are brave enough to try to give the best that's in you.

Friends are sounding boards. They are shoulders to cry on. They are the ones who make you smile and sparkle when you are with them. Friends are always there with aid and sustenance and maybe a flower or two. It might not always be what you want, but it's bound to be what you really need.

A real friend would never seek to influence you to do anything that would bring you physical, emotional, or spiritual harm. They love and respect you too much to ever do that. So note the direction in which others are waving you to proceed. Friendship protects.

For those of us who have experienced a kind of blessed, inspiring, and devoted friendship in our lives—however brief it might have been—we have known a bit of heaven's care for us right here on earth. For those of us who still have these friendships in our lives, it is reason enough to kneel in grateful prayer.

There are many who will slide into our lives who are only "sunny weather friends," as the old song acclaims, but our hearts knew that all along. The heart's divining powers recognize the difference between solid gold and gold plate.

God knows he seems remote and far from our daily rounds of trouble and struggle. It's why he sprinkled our hearts with the twinkling lights of friendships. In enjoining our lights, we all shine brighter.

I believe heaven touches and cares for us through one another.

# 46
# The Pleasant Nature of Gifts

What constitutes a gift? Well, it can be many things. However, I know one thing: a gift is not limited to something that can be wrapped in pretty paper, tucked in a box, put on a credit card, or sent in the mail.

I know that a gift was given to me when someone had such a burst of love or appreciation for me that it caused them to want to do something to make me happy, and they tried to express those feelings in a meaningful way. Maybe I could unwrap what the gift was—or maybe I couldn't.

Cost was never a measure, but energy often was!

Some of my most cherished gifts were kindergarten drawings or wilting wildflowers in a small child's outstretched hand.

So, no matter the item or the act, I can always feel the love that's being shown to me with whatever the gift may be. That's what truly makes my heart smile.

You and I both know that we use the scales of the heart to weigh and measure the gifts that will live on in our memories.

# 47
## Pastor Bob Told Me

Pastor Bob knew I was wrestling with a problem related to a family member who always seemed to be getting in a jam and calling on Jesse and me to bail him out. Finally, after taking note of our efforts for some time, Pastor Bob offered some advice. He said, "Leona, some folks are like those pesky moles we sometimes get in our backyards. They can ruin it with their activity. There's no use thinking that if you throw dirt in his hole on the one end that it will do any good. Because while you're trying to throw dirt in the one end, he's continually digging the hole deeper on the other end. Sometimes you just have to give it up—and get the darn troublemaker out of your yard."

# 48
# The Nectar of Our Moments

I feel we're all reborn with each new day. I remain happy for the most part because I awaken each morning feeling like I have shaken off the shell of yesterday like a butterfly emerging from a cocoon. It is freeing. There's a joyful expectation realizing that there are moments that await me of whose nectar I haven't yet tasted.

Oh, I know not all may be pleasant, but I look for the sweet moments. And they're here—today—growing in the garden of each of our lives. Like me, you should search them out and then savor them. Rest lightly on each sun-filled instant. Let its sweetness bless you.

Why would we choose to chew on the rags of yesterday like a dark moth in the attic when we have the blossoms of today awaiting our discovery.

But, then, it is your day, it is your life, and when you spread your wings over tomorrow, it is your spirit's choice to make. So, I ask you: moth or butterfly?

Leona Flowers

# 49
## *Your Gifts*

Every gift to our inner person that we've been fortunate enough to receive comes with the responsibility to use it as best we can.

Someone called this heavenly philanthropy toward us "the miraculous nature of talent."

Share your gift with as many and as often as life's circumstances will allow, but try to keep its dispersal in balance with your life's other obligations.

It's an important lesson we don't often learn in a timely way.

# 50
# The Lesson of the Bread

I enjoy making a good loaf of healthy bread. I guess it's because I know that what I'll be serving to others will be filled with the kind of stuff that will nourish and satisfy them.

I recall that someone wrote something on the subject, which I read many years ago, about there being "a good sermon in a wholesome loaf of bread" that we share with others because there's kindness and caring revealed in the effort.

You know, despite all the best ingredients we may assemble for baking our bread, without one thing—the yeast—the loaf is unable to become all it should be. I hasten to say the bread will not be worth putting on the table.

I like to think that heaven would want us to be somewhat like the humble yeast wherever we may go among others and prove to be a blessing to those with whom we mingle.

Leona Flowers

# 51
# Don't Be Deceived

Someone pointed out to me years ago that often, from a distance, if the work is good enough, it's hard to tell the difference between an artificial rose and a real one. However, the difference becomes gloriously obvious as we move in for a closer examination of their construction.

With the real, living flower, we become spellbound by its amazing design and detail, its symmetry, the color and shape of each living petal, and so much more. As a modern camera goes deeper and deeper in its discovery of the rose, what we view is unbelievable perfection that awes our senses.

When we approach the man-made creation with the camera lens, the closer we look, the more randomness and flaws we observe in its construction. Just boring disorderliness throughout.

There's a lesson for us in this.

With all things in life, including people, we should look for the real deal—that which is honest and vibrant and won't disappoint us when we move in closer.

We need to keep our eyes open for truth and real beauty and be aware of those things and those people that might deceive us.

# 52

# Don't Regret the Good You've Done

If you were there when someone needed you, and you stood between them and the world … if you cared for them when no one else cared and were their advocate when others accused them … if your arms and door remain open to them, although they see no need for you today … don't weep, my friend, and don't regret the days you gave to loving, aiding, supporting, and lifting others up.

It was your own soul being shaped and led in the doing.

# 53
## *Renewal*

Judge yourselves wisely and well, my friends. Be as fair and reasonable with yourself as you would be with others. The universe wants to lift, heal and rebuild you—not crush you.

It's a good thing to often take an honest inventory of our souls, but when the assessment is done, and you know what needs fixing in your life, forgive yourself as heaven does. Dust yourself off and move forward, unburdened, into the unmarked days that lie before each of us.

Resolve to try harder and do better. Leave yesterday behind with all its sins, sorrows, failings, and demands on your heart and mind. Today's cares require today's strength.

Don't carry into tomorrow the heavy trappings of missteps and mistakes. Your soul must claim and grasp the grace that heaven extends to us whenever our regret is sincere.

How will you adorn yourselves with the new joy and blessings that heaven wants to bestow upon you if you are still clinging to the worn-out robes of yesterday's misery and discontent? A dear pastor friend of mine told me years ago that we never run out of opportunities for beginning again. A successful life is about recognizing the time and need for renewal. It's always only a choice away.

# 54

# *Responding to Need*

My husband, Jesse, and I were talking about the widespread and increasing state of homelessness in our country.

"Homelessness could be any of us without a job or someone to turn to," my husband said.

Yes, life can change for any of us very quickly. For me—who has never been without a home no matter how humble it might have been—seeing folks without one is heartbreaking. The images today of so many people sleeping in cars or on the streets in cardboard boxes is extremely unsettling. As it should be.

We don't know the details or the many burdens and circumstances of living that had the power to pull another person down. We can only see where they have landed. It's not our duty to know *why* someone is in a place of need. The reasons are too many. Our focus should be on the images we see before us that need to be addressed.

I know the work of helping so many homeless people seems overwhelming, but so are floods and fires and earthquakes. Good folks just roll up their sleeves, pick a point somewhere in the problem, and pitch in. Homelessness is just one more work of mercy.

We all know that perfect solutions in humanitarian work aren't possible, but many hands make the work easier. A lot can be accomplished when, together, we direct our efforts toward easing the suffering we see around us every day.

Our acts of helpfulness and charity can be thought of as a kind of a thank-you offering that we contribute to life for our own many blessings—and perhaps for sparing us from what we learn that others are enduring.

You've heard it repeated more than once, I'm sure, about all that is necessary for evil (or suffering in these instances) to triumph is that good people do nothing.

Well, then, let's keep doing something, my friends.

# 55

# Patchwork Philosophy

Patchwork: Something made up of a variety of pieces that may lack a harmony of its parts.

I have a friend who makes the most beautiful quilts from items she picks up in thrift stores. She launders the material, cuts it into squares, and places all the pieces in a special box. Each piece will sit there until her muse informs her that the time has come for each and every piece to find a new role to assume.

That's when the magic begins.

I never fail to be impressed with each finished masterpiece of her handiwork.

When she holds them up before me, it's hard to believe that no one else was able to see the potential for service remaining in each cast-off item or the potential of each to play a role in another person's eventual delight. Even those pieces of material I had thought quite ugly, at first glance, prove to find their place and function in her vision. Her gift for making so much from so little has never failed to inspire me.

As we pass through each life experience, we too are filling our own special boxes of fragments and pieces. We might not see, just yet, the purpose and meaning in each trial, triumph, or circumstance, but considered carefully, wisely, and honestly, you will eventually come to

Leona Flowers

see the role that each and every thing has played in creating the beautiful design of the person that you are today.

For my own part, I look back over a long life filled with both light and dark places and a multitude of people. Most have been bright and beautiful people who colored my days with the joy they shared and the lessons they taught. Whether helpful or hurtful, though, each one of those I have known has left little patches of themselves on the design of my life.

When I look back, I realize that—even with all of our human wisdom—we never know the impact and effect that each experience or each encounter will make upon us. I have to smile knowing there is surely a divine Crafter who is at work in our lives determining how the final product will appear.

# 56
# *Valuable Places*

When I was a small child, I rode happily along on the seat of a horse and wagon. I was never embarrassed that it was our only means of transportation. Our sweet old horse, Sis, carried us along the roads to wherever we needed to go. Most other folks had cars in the 1940s, but Dad couldn't afford one and had never learned to drive anyway.

I loved listening to my dad's stories and songs and fatherly advice as the clop clop clop of Sis's horseshoes resounded on the highway.

That wagon was a happy place for me because I was sitting next to my father. His presence in that place made all the difference in the world to a small girl's measure of things that matter.

The years haven't changed me very much. I still value people and experiences of love and friendship above almost everything else. I've found in life that it's not so much *where* we are that affects us as much as *who* we're with. When I look back, it's the faces that are the precious keepsakes in my thoughts.

Since I married Jesse fifty-six years ago, I've often said that I could live contentedly almost anywhere as long as he was near me—yet no mansion on earth would hold any joy for me without his presence there.

I've known many of my life's most precious moments in humble dwellings with those I've loved and whose dear hearts loved me in return.

I've been rich in my lifetime in everything I felt really mattered, and my heart knows that my father's wagon and my mother's kitchen table are two simple places where I knew the real lasting luxury of the heart.

# 57

# Popeye the Sailor and I

As Popeye said, "I am what I am."

From the time I first heard that statement in a Popeye movie, when I was around seven, I liked the attitude of acceptance and self-approval it presented to my young mind.

My thinking hasn't changed where that's concerned.

Like my old cartoon hero, Popeye, I think it's always better to come to grips with *who* you are in all your complexity and imperfections than to try to be some fabrication of a you for social or career purposes—or perhaps just because you've been influenced to believe you're missing something.

My mom helped me with a teenage angst I briefly experienced over image and acceptance by reminding me that I would never find acceptance and approval from all of those who I wanted it to come from. Be happy, she advised, with those who honestly enjoyed my company. Be myself, and the friends I would find would be a good mix.

She was right, of course. I still sometimes wonder why I've enjoyed all the marvelous friendships and all the affection that have blessed my life. I guess being the same person each time we meet may have made it easier on folks. I've grown, but I never outgrew my basic nature. If my jokes didn't suit you fifty years ago, they haven't improved that much.

I recognize the years have done what the years will do, and I'm now an elaboration of my youthful self. But the me I am today is still identifiable to anyone who has ever known me at any stage in my life.

You could ask my older brother, Donald, or my husband, Jesse, or any of my old chums (who still have a good memory of anything at all), and they'll verify that despite the fact that I'm a little bit battle-scarred, I still own my own voice the very same as I did at fifteen or forty—or any year on the calendar—and I'm still as enthusiastic about life as ever.

My point, friends, is that we should all grow in knowledge, wisdom, perspective, and character, but if you're past forty years old and you're still wondering who you are, or who you should be, well, I think Popeye would say that you've missed the chance to have been living your best life all along—simply as yourself.

I've seen an awful lot of people in my seventy-nine years, but I've never found anyone else I'd rather be than *me*. It's made life so much simpler and easier to live. Maybe that's what Popeye and I have had in common all along.

# 58
# When Life Calls Me

Between the early-morning hours
and when I end my day,
the whole of life is mine to share.
I have a role in all that is
and know that even pain
can speak to me in message clear:
"I'm here."
I rise up, and I lie down,
and in between,
life turns the wheel of time for me.
Its tragic magic draws me
into who knows where,
and yet I'm here.
A rainbow, a dewdrop,
a kiss on my lips,
my heart on a celestial ride.
I tried to stay sad when things were so bad,
I did, I really tried,
But life wouldn't let me
loose of its grip
when I tried to sink under the tide.
It kept tossing me lines
of thoughts so divine

that I had to rise up
and I sighed.
The flowers of love
that get tossed
at my feet
find a place in my lovely bouquet,
and though I may seek
that long-lasting sleep,
sweet voices urge me to stay.
I am where I am
where life placed me.
In my thoughts, my nature, and time,
like a character in a celestial play
where just author knows reason
and rhyme.
Between the hours
of sunrise and dark,
I dance a path down
through the years.
Awesome and grand
is the music of life,
which drowns out
my groanings and tears.
My soul is held fast
in a web spun of joy.
My breath a mysterious design,
I cannot but gasp,
"I am here, I am here,
in this glorious place and in time."

# 59
## *Surviving It All*

Perhaps, like me, you've discovered that there's no use looking back and longing for a place in your life that no longer exists and that you can't expect others—no matter how much they love you—to be able to take you there.

Perhaps, like me, you've had tsunamis of loss and grief that ravaged the person you once were before the loss or the pain took you down.

Perhaps, when the tears subsided and the restless heart within you quieted, you knew that the world and all of life had forever changed.

But perhaps in time, your mind assessed the resources remaining to you—like the love still waiting for you, the arms that reach to lift you, the lessons and voices within your memory that have always proven enabling and true—and you slowly began to rise, take your place once more among others, and rebuild and restore a stronger shelter for your soul. And so, we go on.

# A Message to My Readers

Thanks for taking the time to read my book. I hope you found something of value within its pages.

Today, Jesse and I live in Florida. Our three remaining children live near us, and we enjoy many happy times together.

Jesse and I are never lonely. Far from it! Our several levels of grandchildren fill our lives with joy and laughter. Our phones ring often, and text messages are a continuous part of our days. Great-grandchildren let us see and hear them in video chats. How could we not be happy?

I'm as busy now with family as I ever was—and maybe more so since the older grandchildren are in their thirties and forties and include us in their interesting and successful lives.

We're among those who know that it's true that grandchildren help keep you feeling young and staying active. Mine are also wonderful reservoirs of memories of each portion of my life that I spent with them.

Jesse and my life took quite a remarkable turn a few years ago when our daughter Merry and her husband Michael Teller enrolled their youngest son, Miles, in NYU's acting school. His exceptional talent was noted while there, and before graduating, he got his first acting role in a film called *Rabbit Hole*. His career took off splendidly and today he's been described as an "A" lister! As a result of his success we have gotten to meet and develop friendships with many marvelous people in the entertainment industry who we would never have gotten to know otherwise. Today, many are dear and close friends. Huffpost has even referred to me as "the world's coolest grandma." and "the favorite of the famous." Statements like these make me smile.

When I reflect, as these essays show, on my often hard and challenging past, I know that I had to have *begun* as I did and *traveled* where I've been led, over just such a path as mine, in order to recognize how amazing my journey has truly been. It's been quite an incredible tale.

Who would have ever believed that a once barefoot child who played with a pig called Sally would someday go to Hollywood premieres? Or that she would write a book?

I smile when I think that if the memorable gypsy grandma I met in my childhood who I've written about in Time and Tea Leaves (1) had told me that someday I would have grandchildren who were so remarkable that one was capable of earning a master's degree while holding two jobs as she and her husband raised three small children, that another would be so sharp that she'd become a self-made millionaire, that one would be a high school dropout yet earn a scholarship to Columbia University, and that another would become a famous actor who has had his photo taken with the president of the United States—and mentioned my several other ones who are each worthy of my pride in their achievements, I probably would have found it all just too impossible to believe.

Well, to tell the truth, I'm kind of glad she couldn't see all this back then. I've probably enjoyed these occurrences more so because it has all taken me by such spectacular surprise.

In summary, dear reader, I'm grateful beyond words for those *of my own* family who have lovingly called me "Mom" and "Grandma." But I also hold a sweet affection for the many others who have found in me a source of some valued grandmotherly wisdom. I've been delighted when my grandson Miles has told television audiences that I'm "like everybody's grandma—or at least the kind of grandma they wished they had." It always warms my heart when he says it.

I'm so happy he feels that way. I'll continue to try and prove him right. Thanks again.

Leona Flowers

Made in the USA
Columbia, SC
02 July 2022